LEADERSHIP INTELLIGENCE

LEADERSHIP INTELLIGENCE

The 5Qs for Thriving as a Leader

ALI QASSIM JAWAD AND ANDREW KAKABADSE

BLOOMSBURY BUSINESS

LONDON · NEW YORK · OXFORD · NEW DELHI · SYDNEY

BLOOMSBURY BUSINESS
Bloomsbury Publishing Plc
50 Bedford Square, London, WC1B 3DP, UK
1385 Broadway, New York, NY 10018, USA

BLOOMSBURY, BLOOMSBURY BUSINESS and the Diana logo are trademarks
of Bloomsbury Publishing Plc

First published in Great Britain 2019

Cover design by Jason Anscomb / Rawshock Design

A catalogue record for this book is available from the British Library.

A catalog record for this book is available from the Library of Congress.

ISBN: HB: 978-1-4729-6392-5
ePDF: 978-1-4729-6394-9
eBook: 978-1-4729-6393-2

Typeset by Newgen KnowledgeWorks Pvt. Ltd., Chennai, India
Printed and bound in Great Britain

To find out more about our authors and books visit www.bloomsbury.com
and sign up for our newsletters.

CONTENTS

MQ is a leader's ability to understand their own value system
and draw on this to determine the moral boundaries of
individuals, teams and of the organization.

ACKNOWLEDGEMENTS

Special Thank you

We are deeply grateful to all the ministers of state, CEOs, chairmen, general managers, middle- and lower-level managers, public servants, politicians and the managers and employees of third-sector organisations, for their inspiration, views and comments on leadership that have led to this book. Working with you, coaching and counselling you, consulting with you and researching you has provided the thinking and evidence that has made the 5Qs concept a reality. All of you are special as each of you has provided a unique insight, which we have drawn upon to shape this book.

Special mention is due to His Majesty Sultan Qaboos bin Said, Head of State, Sultan of Oman. Oman is a geographically vast country with a small population, fairly modest natural resources and complicated neighbours. Despite this, Oman is politically unassuming and has managed to become a byword for stability, tolerance and sensible neutrality. How did Oman pull it off? The answer is *leadership*, and we hope this book captures how.

The fact that Sultan Qaboos bin Said is still revered by the population after nearly half a century in power is remarkable.

A high IQ has clearly been needed. Running a company is demanding; running a country even more so. Running a country with a complex cultural make-up is even harder. Running it successfully for nearly half a century is an astounding achievement, one that requires a leader with a high degree of cognitive intelligence to be able to devise, maintain and adapt his arguments in the face of new and evolving challenges.

But IQ is not enough. Sultan Qaboos's understanding of himself and of his very diverse citizens led him to realize that what others saw as a challenge was actually an opportunity to build a stronger nation. A keen sense of others' concerns, insecurities and aspirations, coupled with a good understanding of one's own emotions and with having a good grip on them, emotional intelligence (EQ), complements IQ, inspiring a way forward.

Political intelligence (PQ) is also important. The sultanate's careful navigation of the contrasting agendas of its fellow members of the Gulf Corporation Council (GCC) and other regional and global powers, such as Iran, the United States, China, India and the United Kingdom has required a highly attuned political instinct and steadfast determination to engage the different stakeholders. Charting a way forward through diverse stakeholders' agendas while ensuring continued engagement with critical players, has been a distinct feature of his reign.

His resilience (RQ) has also been evident. Sultan Qaboos did not lose sight of his goals despite facing economic pressures such as a drop in the price of exports, or political pressure when the geopolitical fault lines yawn wide enough to trigger a severe diplomatic rift.

A further interesting fact suggests there is more at work. In 2015 the International Centre for the Study of Radicalisation and Political Violence at London's King's College found that not a single Omani had joined the more than 20,000 foreign fighters battling alongside

Islamic State of Iraq and Syria (ISIS). In November 2016, the Sydney-based Institute for Economics and Peace released its annual Global Terrorism Index, which assesses the impact of terrorism on 163 countries on a scale of zero to ten. Just 34 countries scored zero, and Oman was the only country in the Middle East among them.

This is not the result of chance. It is the result of moral leadership (MQ). It is the presence of an unwavering moral compass has allowed Sultan Qaboos to have a clear vision from the very beginning of his reign of what he wanted his country to be. He started by empowering women at the same time as overcoming an inherited insurgency and uniting the sometimes fractious tribes behind his vision. Clarity about where his moral compass points and his staying true to it have made Oman into a peaceful nation with a cohesive society and a strong sense of nationhood.

The concept of the 5Qs outlined in this book, and its underlying ideas, form the basis of the Omani National Programme on Competitiveness and Citizen Wellbeing, bringing together government and the private sector in partnership to realize ambitious national goals. This by itself is a welcome acclaim.

So thank you again. We'd like to dedicate this book to the men and women who have provided living examples of what well-rounded leadership can be. What we as authors have learnt from you is that these principles are universal. They can be applied to the running of companies, to governments, to multilateral institutions. Distilling and codifying the principles of the 5Qs is the purpose of this book. We hope it will contribute to your own success by providing a framework for your continued development.

Dr Ali Qassim Jawad

I wish to thank my loving and supportive wife, Yasmin, and my six wonderful children, Eman, Zahra, Mona, Adam, Amal and Ibrahim, for their continuous love and inspiration.

I also wish to thank H. E. Sayed Khalid bin Hilal Al-Busaidi, Minister of the Diwan of Royal Court, for his guidance, support and encouragement throughout this project.

Prof Andrew Kakabadse

I wish to thank my wife, Professor Nada Kakabadse, for all her help, love, support and continual advice on this book. Thank you also to Sophia and Reeves. Having watched you as the next generation on how you face up to and address the challenges confronting you, it is clear that the concept of the 5Qs spans geography and generations. Without knowing it, your input to my thinking has been invaluable.

FOREWORD

It is better to lead from behind and to put others in front, especially when you celebrate victory, when nice things occur. You take the front line when there is danger. Then people will appreciate your leadership . . . There are times when a leader must move out ahead of the flock, go off in a new direction, confident that he is leading his people the right way.

NELSON MANDELA

Leadership was something I (Peter Hain) learnt on the job.

Nobody taught me how to be an anti-apartheid campaign leader as I found myself thrust into doing when I was aged nineteen. Still less two decades later was I tutored to be a member of parliament and subsequently a government and then cabinet minister.

Yet the experience gained in this unique journey from protestor to peer during fifty years in politics has enabled me to teach MBA students and apply the lessons I've learnt to businesses and other organizations.

It has been both a privilege and a great responsibility entrusted to me to lead others to achieve success, perhaps the most important one being negotiating the 2007 settlement to the Northern Ireland conflict, which brought bitter old enemies into self-government together.

Experience and wisdom from others often guided me, but mostly I learnt leadership by myself, including from my own errors.

Outstanding leaders are powerful in communication, agile in response to changing circumstances, good at listening, willing to keep learning – and yet resilient. Perhaps, most of all, great leaders can think and rethink quickly as circumstances change.

Whether as cabinet minister, chair or CEO, making things happen through smart actions is necessary. But where are the texts that capture how to work through demanding challenges and draw on the skills and qualities that make a difference?

Perhaps this book can fill that gap. Based on their extensive global research embracing many thousands of organizations and three governments, the authors conclude that five separate intelligences underpin the outstanding leader.

Cognitive intelligence (IQ) is often considered the critical one. But in a world of misalignments and people pursuing contrasting – sometimes competing – interests, thinking fast on one's feet and coming up with a compelling argument is an absolute must. Unless other people are actually listening and are persuaded, of what value are other leadership skills and qualities?

Clarity of perspective is vital, but by itself, not sufficient. Engaging with others, capturing their imagination, making people feel that their concerns and desires are central to what is being proposed, goes hand in hand with clever thinking. That brings in the widely quoted emotional intelligence (EQ) – in many ways the soft side to the sharp mind.

But that is also insufficient. The skills of political intelligence (PQ) are also necessary to secure cohesion in a world of growing differences. Being sensitive (EQ) and being a clever negotiator (PQ) overlap; PQ is like EQ but with an agenda and that is what it takes to turn the impossible into a possible.

Those who take charge handle differences and tensions, which after a while can wear you down. Thus, the fourth Q, the resilience quotient (RQ); resilience is being emotionally tough inside and yet responsive and understanding on the outside – not an easy combination to achieve, but a vital one.

Yet, in a world of exposure to press, media and social media, what value the 4Qs without that clear moral compass? The fifth Q, the moral quotient (MQ), steers leaders through dilemmas they inevitably face. Dilemmas are the prerogative and privilege of leaders. Great leaders not only carve ways forward, but are also the last line of defence. Knowing where you stand and why is as important as clever thinking and sensitive behaviour. As a leader, you know you have arrived by the increasing dilemmas you have had to face.

And so the 5Qs. This innovative book captures sharpness of intellect with warmth and responsiveness; strength of character to persist; and an ethical guide through moral turbulence.

It may be suggested that each of these leadership intelligences have already been outlined in some way or other across many different literatures, from policy, strategy, sociology and psychology to philosophy.

But for the first time these vast fields have been condensed into a readable, slim volume outlining the five intelligences of leadership that make the distinct difference to the performance and contribution of any leader.

There are no easy steps to leadership. This is a book both for leaders who wish to keep improving and those who want to become leaders.

Adopting the 5Qs will help you navigate through some of the most challenging leadership terrains you are ever likely to meet.

The son of South African activists forced into exile when he was a teenager in 1966, Lord Peter Hain was a British anti-apartheid leader, then MP for Neath 1991–2015; secretary of state successively for Northern Ireland, Wales, Work and Pensions, Leader of the House of Commons and a former Foreign Office Minister of State and Energy Minister. The author of twenty-one books, his memoirs Outside In were published by Biteback in 2012. A visiting fellow of Henley Business School, he is also a visiting professor at Wits Business School and University of South Wales.

Introduction

Improving performance was the only issue on the agenda for the meeting. Keep it simple and focused, thought the HR director John as he made his opening statement: 'We need to be clear on what our unique competitive advantage is, and then build the skills and capabilities to achieve this'.

He looked around the table. The other centre and business head directors appeared to agree. And yet fifteen minutes later John was powerless as the meeting rapidly deteriorated into turf wars. Every time some progress was made, defensiveness took over. Self-protection. Self-preservation.

All agreed that the company's unique competitive advantage was service. But then costs and budgets reared their disruptive heads. Headquarters stood in the way, John's colleagues said time and time again.

Yet, none would give way when it came to their budgets and organization. At the same time, each denied not being a team player.

John looked around the room and could see his hard work over the last six months evaporating. What can you do when faced with incompatible perspectives and no willingness to adjust?

This scenario might sound familiar. Such meetings are as commonplace as they are confusing. Global business has become complex, and everyday interactions are often characterized by a lack of harmony as individuals relentlessly pursue their own agendas, often for good reason. The challenge this book addresses is how we can do a much better job of advancing our own personal and organizational challenges by becoming aligned and engaged in the midst of a world of diverse opinions and actions.

Navigating through disturbing complexities is at the heart of modern management – whether in a corporation, a hospital or a government department. Yet, there is little discussion about making political interactions a core management skill. Bookshelves groan under the weight of books about strategy, and the qualities of the great leader who will produce motivated and dedicated followers. Management literature is full of debate on how pulling together and going in the same direction is a must-have capability. The assumption seems to be that, if we talk about a problem long enough, everyone will see the underlying logic and come to a shared conclusion.

Such rational thinking is powerful and goes back to the 1920s when the Chicago School of Economics promoted 'economic rationalism'. This concept suggested that if you establish a clear and rational picture that all can agree is true, then everyone will subsequently engage with it. In so doing, everyone's interests will neatly align. The philosophy of rationalism is deep and goes back to Sir Isaac Newton, gravity and the powerful tradition of scientific measurement that followed. Scientific rationalism within 200 years morphed into economic rationalism, which embraces and often suffocates organizations today.

Rationalism only gets you so far in the hugely complex and perplexingly human world of the modern organization. The banking crisis of the mid-2000s was just one example of how objectivity is very much in the eye of the beholder. What is needed instead is diversity of thinking. The complexities of organizations have to be tackled by nimble minds which can manage not only what an organization *should* be but also, more importantly, what its value delivery *is* and *could* be.

Value delivery lies at the heart of organizations. For those who manage them, it requires as great an investment of time as strategy creation or execution. Success necessitates understanding the logic of what needs to be done combined with the contextual sensitivity to ensure something happens. In tandem this overcomes all the emotional, egotistical and cultural obstacles that prevent success.

This was John's problem. All of the directors agreed that a company-wide strategy for competitive advantage was eminently sensible. 'There's no need to go over it all again, John. We've bought in', exclaimed one of the directors. In reality, however, as John surveyed his colleagues, there was no buy-in. There was little chance of making the agreed service strategy work. The different parts of the organization would react differently when faced with the challenge of responding to the demands of the market.

Two leadership mindsets

Over decades of working with organizations across the world, we have concluded that there are two very different approaches to creating value as a leader. One is about 'pursuing a value proposition' and the other is about 'delivered value'. We believe strongly in the latter approach.

The creator of a value proposition is more likely to be a big picture thinker who elevates strategy above all else. The creator of delivered value, in contrast, is characterized by closeness to customers and other stakeholders – and bases their strategy on the evidence they provide. Another way of expressing this difference is to say that some leaders are vision based – they have a (largely untested) vision of how value can be created, and some are mission based – focused on the delivery of evidence-based value.

Most leaders have a default setting, leaning towards one of these mindsets: perceived or delivered value.

Those who champion value proposition thinking (vision-based leadership) start by formulating a perceived value or hypothesis, and then look for evidence to support their strategy. They have a preconceived notion of how the organization can create value and enact a strategy to achieve it. Usually, the strategy emanates from inside the boardroom. Typical visions are being the biggest, the best, the most powerful, the most dominant in the market.

Unfortunately, achieving the vision may become an end in itself. Witness the problems experienced by both Toyota and Volkswagen once they decided to pursue a vision of being the biggest car manufacturers (and before them General Motors). In both cases, previously well-run companies took their eye off the ball, losing sight of the mission that had made them great in the first place. The value they perceived would flow from being the biggest in their markets failed to materialize.

With the perceived value approach, there is a danger that strategy will become dogma as senior managers aim to justify a preconceived view of the world and value creation. Value creation may become uncoupled from reality and from the evidence that supports it. Routine and denial take over and the organization runs on pre-existing competence for some time rather than on excellence, but ultimately is doomed to failure.

There is another way. Effective mission-based leaders gather evidence from stakeholders inside and outside to determine the value the organization is delivering today and can deliver in the future. A strategy is then put in place to support these findings and is deliberately exposed to challenges from stakeholders to create engagement. These are value delivery-driven organizations.

Connecting the dots of reality on a daily and dynamic basis is the foundation to truly delivering value. Companies that are successful over many years find ways to instil what they stand for and their approach into the acts of value creation and delivery.

Leaders focused on delivered value strive to create a culture that constantly interrogates the evidence to test the strategy. These sorts of leaders are driven by value creation among stakeholders outside of the boardroom and focus on proving their strategy every day with the evidence gathered.

Yet our research suggests that the majority of leaders fall into the first category, holding a value proposition mindset. Perceived value rules. Boardrooms are full of executives pursuing a predetermined view with very little desire to adapt, or perhaps even to listen to evidence. A complex network of incompatible logics often saturates the very fabric of the boardroom.

Cutting through the complexity

The purpose of this book is to help leaders become successful at working through complexities to achieve an aligned view and to convince people to focus on value delivery.

The measure and true task of any good leader is their ability to constantly challenge assumptions around value creation and what needs to be done to support the organization's mission.

We are not suggesting it is easy. Organizational leaders work in complex, technology-rich, fast-paced environments and economies, struggling to deal with previously non-existent challenges. Contemporary governance calls for a varied and versatile cognitive approach to problems. Demanding times require nimble minds.

Paul Polman, chief executive of Unilever, commenting on CEO success, observes,[1] 'The average CEO tenure is now 4½ years; the average lifetime of a publicly traded company is now 17 years. The qualities leaders possessed in the past may not be applicable to the future.

'The challenges we are seeing right now differ significantly from the challenges that were there 10, 20, or 30 years ago. We are living in a very interesting time when economic, environmental and geopolitical risks and technology revolutions are all coming together. Clearly some people have a hard time dealing with that.

'One of the most important character traits of a leader today is courage. I work on a lot of sustainable development goals and we are working on poverty alleviation, sustainable farming or climate change

---

[1]*Sunday Times*, 18 September 2017, page 12 (Appointments).

and I often find myself on panels with highly specialized people – who are sometimes also highly critical people. Sometimes it's difficult as the CEO to be that knowledgeable but you have to have the courage to participate'.

Poleman is describing the new reality of leadership. Many of our most talented managers and potential leaders are singularly ill-equipped to meet these challenges at present. We hope this book will help them.

Our research has identified that high-performing leaders simultaneously employ five key leadership intelligences, referred to as the 5Qs, to achieve effective transformational change and to deeply embed this change in order to have sustainable success.

The 5Qs are cognitive intelligence (IQ); emotional intelligence (EQ); political intelligence (PQ); resilience quotient (RQ): and moral intelligence (MQ). Much as DNA's constituent nucleic acids create the substance that works as the framework for human life, these 5Qs come together to inform every aspect of leadership.

Distilled to their essence,

- IQ is a leader's ability to acquire knowledge, reflecting their deductive/rationalist abilities and drawing together contrasting strands of information to emerge with a compelling argument that entices;

- EQ is a leader's ability to understand and manage both their own emotions, and those of others;

- PQ is a leader's ability to navigate a way forward through diverse stakeholders' agendas while ensuring continued engagement with critical players;

- RQ reflects the capacity of a leader to emotionally sustain high performance under continued pressure and adversity (It includes the courage and strength of character to participate referred to by Polman.); and

- MQ is a leader's ability to understand their own value system and draw on this to determine the moral boundaries of individuals, teams and of the organization.

These intelligences represent the unconscious and conscious controls on the actions we take to shape our response to external demands.

It may seem counterintuitive to argue, as we do in this book, that creating delivered value requires political intelligence (PQ) as well as IQ. Politics is often viewed as a negative force. We talk about office politics as toxic to a culture. But in its true meaning, politics is the process by which different, often competing, interests are reconciled to achieve a positive change. PQ is the antidote to complexity. It is one of the Five Qs – along with IQ, EQ, RQ and MQ – that mission-based leaders require.

Our studies tested these concepts on elite leaders including ministers, top civil servants, C-level and board executives in the United States, the United Kingdom, India, Australia, Europe, Russia, Asia and the Gulf region, and were applied at four critical levels of leadership: lower management; general management; top team; and board.

These organizational levels represent the skills required for particular work domains, namely different clusters of work practices, where demands range from relatively simple tasks and activities that require rational thinking and teamwork at the delivery level, through to the complex positioning of concepts and subtle influencing of stakeholders at top team and board levels.

Think of a visa processor in the ministry of foreign affairs in the former case, and the foreign minister himself in the latter. Leaders working at different levels, and work domains require different combinations of the 5Qs.

The 5Qs vary in implementation across different organizations and change according to seniority and the strategic and operational considerations faced.

Our research highlights that the 5Qs are not consistently practised across these four management levels.

While an ever greater level of IQ appears necessary at each level, the degree to which leaders are required to utilize their PQ appears to increase as they rise through the organizational hierarchy. In contrast, leaders draw most on their EQ at lower management and general management, but less at the top team and board levels.

High-performing strategic leaders possess the ability to analyse and skilfully handle conflicting agendas, for example between IQ and PQ. Being a team player is important but not critical at this level. In government especially, a high degree of PQ and EQ allows civil servants to best understand the interests and reactions of all the involved parties – the most important being the citizenry. It is incumbent for both the minister and the civil servant to find ways through conflicting demands and to emerge with a viable policy and provide services for the public. The citizen may not know what is the right policy, but they can quickly sense when they are not being well served.

Looking at this more closely, it could be said that IQ, EQ and PQ are 'value free' intelligences. A leader with high cognitive, emotional and political quotients can apply these for good or bad purposes. Moral intelligence, in contrast, is by definition 'value led' and provides a checking function or conscience in decision-making. It is odd to report that the higher one moves in the organization, the less ethical and moral the practices become, irrespective of what is said publicly. (This controversial point is discussed further in the MQ chapter.)

While the question of whether IQ is inherited or developed over time is debatable, the evidence suggests that EQ, PQ and MQ can all be cultivated throughout a lifetime or over a career. A leadership model that emphasizes the nurturing of these intelligences will serve to fill serious gaps in the next generation and help develop a balanced and informed thinking framework for addressing strategy, governance and policy problems.

In a world where the political, social and economic landscape changes rapidly and without warning, all leaders – private, third and public sector – must possess the fundamental building blocks that ensure sustainable results. These are the 5Qs.

Ali Qassim Jawad and Andrew Kakabadse

1

IQ: Thinking your way to competitive advantage

The key item on the board's agenda was the purchase of a power plant in Budapest, Hungary. The CEO and the top team were acquisition hungry. After the finance director finished making the case to the board, the non-executive directors began asking questions. Some felt the case was weak, but the CEO and finance director were impressively persuasive. Their argument was supported with convincing evidence. It looked as if the board was in favour.

At this point the chairperson intervened. She captured the essence of the argument. She knew the details intimately and then clearly, step by step, described the bigger picture. The more the chairperson spoke, the clearer it became that she was not in favour of the acquisition, but she did leave that impression without appearing to offer an opinion. By cleverly using data, she painted a different strategic alternative. She spoke without notes or supporting documents, but the case she made was even more compelling than that put forward by the CEO and finance director, 'So yes, it is a great idea. But what about the management time needed to get this ailing plant up to our standards?

And what do we know about its culture? What sort of government contacts can we leverage and do we have these in Hungary? And if things do not quite work out, what about the risk to our reputation?' The chairperson looked around the board. 'Time to decide!'

Selective and clever use of data, clarity of thinking and a well-rounded argument are all elements of a compelling case. In this instance, the chairperson won the day even though the power plant was cheaply priced.

After the meeting, the chairperson cautiously suggested to the CEO, 'Perhaps next time you and I should spend time thinking through important projects before anything is put to the board. After all, we all want the same thing.'

The chairperson was smart and managed to get her way sensitively but persuasively through force of argument. She is not alone. The upper echelons of organizations are filled with very smart people. They appreciate that how an argument is positioned and that making sense of all the pieces of information presented can make the difference when it comes to winning people over or losing them completely.

IQ is *the* vital skill when working through conflicting data in order to put forward a clear case and argue which direction should be taken next. IQ is associated with factors ranging from morbidity through to mortality, social status and, to a significant degree, biological parental IQ.

The validity of IQ as a predictor of performance in the workplace varies between different types of jobs. Some studies claim that IQ only accounts for a sixth of the variation in income, because many studies are based on young adults who have not yet reached their peak earning capacity, or even completed their education. Our studies say the opposite. Without a deliberate ever-evolving capacity for deduction and rationalization, no top manager is going to last long. IQ is the core skill of management. Each individual needs to develop an ever-greater capacity to think through the challenging complexities they face. Being a top manager demands understanding of strategy, operations, marketing, finance, psychology, teamwork, governance and the list goes on. Appreciating how others think; penetrating their mindset; recognizing why certain relationships and interactions are what they are – these are all elements of the very practical IQ required of managers. Being able to explain why the organization is as it is, and how to move forward next, are key capabilities of any high-performing manager. In so doing they jump between granular detail and grand statement while providing evidence of how the two are linked.

IQ and extra value

'The major challenge I face is dealing with and managing uncertainty. This includes, for example, political, financial, technological and cultural uncertainties, among others. I need to be able to deal with sudden and major issues as they arise, while also continuing to meet our organization's overall goals', one CEO confided.

IQ determines how effectively leaders think about realizing extra value from their roles. It is this that determines how far the leader can position the organization to outperform competitors. The concentrated cognitive abilities that make the difference include

- analytical reasoning

- being responsive to change

- the ability to handle ambiguity

- big-picture thinking

- the setting and aligning of strategies and agendas

- strategic foresight and a long-term vision

Leaders are continually required to draw on their IQ in order to understand highly complex issues. They have to handle uncertainty, develop strategies to effectively address complexities and conflicts, align strategies to objectives, respond to evolving circumstances and changing contexts, and successfully navigate a path forward through contrasting agendas to achieve desired goals.

The number one skill required from all levels of management is the ability to construct and put forward a credible and compelling argument. IQ is about how you see a situation, analyse current circumstances and then use this data to build a model of what to do next and to make your actions credible.

The need for IQ becomes greater the more senior an individual is within an organization. It is those leaders who are confronted with a lack of alignment or seemingly impossible circumstances beyond their control. For those leaders, complexity is a fact of life.

For example, leaders who have made the transition from private- to public-sector roles quickly become conscious of the need to adapt their behaviours and realign goals. This understanding of the broader objectives that drive government includes meeting both social and economic agendas, and the different – and sometimes conflicting – interests and dynamics of a diverse stakeholder network.

The chief operating officer (COO) of one public-sector organization explained that a major adjustment when making the transition from the private sector is recognizing that decision-making processes in the public sector are more complex and time consuming. Understanding this, the reasons for it and adapting behaviour to this new dynamic are crucial to the transition process.

Leaders also need to learn quickly and determine how best to apply the knowledge they have gained in the private sector to the government sector, and also how best to use their intelligence to solve new and unfamiliar problems in order to effectively lead.

Past experience and successes are important. These provide leaders with confidence in their abilities, place them in a strong position to assess the risks associated with future challenges and strategies, and gain them credibility and trust with those they lead or are required to influence in order to bring about change.

Complexity demands IQ

Complex global corporations are not a uniform proposition. They contain an array of often competing stakeholders. If you are a general manager (GM) stationed in Asia, why should you have any understanding or sympathy with your colleagues in North America operating in a market which is mature and saturated? What if an executive team in Chicago is driving a perception of competitive advantage which has little relevance in China?

In organization after organization we have wondered how different it would be if they had a senior management team with joined-up relationships with each other and with the company's operations elsewhere in the world. IQ is a big element in achieving that. Where there is a misalignment of notions of value and competitive advantages, IQ reconciles the differences.

Look at the role of GMs. They are continually attempting to reconcile contrasting logics. That is the job. The GM is often caught between not playing a part in strategy thinking and creation, and being accountable for strategy implementation. In effect they are caught between the demands of top management and of having to justify their actions to customers and middle managers. The plight of the GM is even more difficult when they disagree with the strategy pushed down from on high and then have to ensure middle managers to pursue a strategy few agree with. It is this tension that makes GMs the true barometer of the organization. Because of their proximity to the market, they know what strategies will work or not. Also, due to their seniority, most are well versed in putting together meaningful strategies. What is disturbing is how few top managers consult their GMs on the viability of the strategies being considered or pursued.

What we have observed is that mission-based organizations are much better at this than vision-based organizations. This makes sense. Mission-based (value delivery) leaders are interested in what can be delivered and are more inclined to listen and consult with the people who have to make the strategy work in practice. They tend to be more open to thinking through complexity, supported by evidence for strategy, organizational structures, outsourcing and so on. Vision-based leaders, who pursue a value proposition, are less inclined to engage with the managers who deliver or implement the strategy, believing that the vision is more important than the execution.

In 2004, the Turkish-born GM of a well-known American bank accurately predicted the global financial crisis, which eventually unravelled in front of disbelieving eyes four years later. He held discussions with the CEO on how a change of strategy would minimize the oncoming financial exposure. 'I told him we would lose a couple of billion dollars, and this, as I later explained, we did.' His argument was well constructed and persuasive. If anything, it was too persuasive.

He outlined to the CEO how to repackage the bank's assets and present a new set of offerings to the market. The CEO, and also chairperson of the board, consulted with the board's lead independent director. The director, a former politician (in fact, a former US secretary of state) recommended sacking the GM. 'If he continues this way, our sales force will lose confidence in our products', he said by way of explanation.

The CEO acknowledged the danger of the GM making his views more widely known, but countered that 'we need his brains because what he says is true'. The CEO asked the GM to reposition some of the bank's assets without endangering the current strategy. This he did, and quite successfully.

By 2008, the bank did lose in the global financial crisis, but its losses were measured in hundreds of millions rather than billions of dollars. Senior managers acknowledged that without the Turkish GM, the bank could have been bankrupted. Today the GM is a senior executive vice president, a member of the top team. His sharp, analytical mind is deeply respected.

Teamthink

At the top team level, complexity becomes much greater and so the IQ requirement reaches its maximum demand point. To add to the complication, top teams tend not to behave like teams. The top team in an organization is the meeting point of different, and sometimes conflicting, interests. These have to be negotiated and aligned.

Typically, the nature of the organization's competitive advantage is determined at the top team level. This is easy to say but no easy matter to do. For an international, multi-product or multi-service corporation, different notions of competitive advantage may be held by different top team members. As we have discussed, what competitive advantage means for China may be something quite different for South America, even for the same product range. The corporate centre perspective of competitive advantage may again be different when accounting for the core values and reputation of the organization.

For the John Lewis Partnership in the UK service is core to its competitive advantage. For the US company Caterpillar, it is quality. These two organizations have given extensive thought and attention to their service and quality missions and made them meaningful to those inside the company and to the myriad of external stakeholders. The majority of companies cannot boast such clarity and depth of identity in the theory and execution of their competitive advantage. In fact, our research shows that over 34 per cent of the world's corporations do not hold a shared view on strategy, vision or mission. That is, more than one-third of companies is worth pausing to think about.

These organizations are bedevilled by colleagues pushing forward their perspective on competitive advantage at the expenses of colleagues' views, resulting in infighting, which seriously damages the enterprise. Add to this exposure to the threats of reputational damage and moral conflict should such tensions surface in public. All this takes place while still driving business forward, which means the IQ challenges are higher than ever.

Strategy and IQ

The creation and execution of strategy, any strategy, requires IQ of the highest order. The survival, growth and prosperity of any organization depend on the quality and viability of the strategy the organization is pursuing. Almost inevitably, the longer-term decline of any organization can be directly attributed to poorly developed strategies or, more likely, to clever strategy, poorly executed.

It is difficult to develop consistent, relevant and all-embracing strategies due to the following reasons:

1. A large number of factors have to be considered, including changes in technology, market demands, the actions of competitors, costs, world politics and social tension. Managers need to have sufficient information and high IQ to deal with each of these factors and weld them together into an overall plan.

2. There are challenges of strategy implementation. No matter how well thought-through and valuable one's plans are,

implementing them requires particular skills and approaches to ensure success. By their very nature, strategic plans upset the status quo unless there is a deliberate intention to maintain current conditions. New strategies may necessitate a reorganization of management structures and systems, meaning that people with certain skills or experience are no longer required, making way for new people with fresh ideas. Therefore, in the implementation of a strategy, resistance is common – strife, conflict and disagreement abound, and uncertainty about the future increases. This process has to be handled sensitively in order for the organization to progress.

Every organization pursues some sort of strategy. Key decision makers will make choices, act on contingencies and consider developments in the external environment before making decisions. Whether these choices, actions and understanding form a sensible strategy depends on three key issues:

1. factors influencing strategy

2. key elements of strategy

3. approaches to formulating strategy

The combination of these three issues determines whether an appropriate or inappropriate strategy is generated.

To implement any strategy successfully, managers must confront three crucial problems:

1. Is the strategy workable? Specifically, has attention been given to the reality of what works in the organization and its relevance to the markets?

2. Can the organization call upon the necessary resources for effective strategy implementation?

3. Will key people in the organization support the strategies?

The issue of resources is relatively easy to resolve (in theory). Resources can be bought in by hiring new labour, purchasing equipment, acquiring a competitor, going to the markets for funding or borrowing from banks. The decision will depend on market and industry trends, and also on expectations for the organization's future performance in the marketplace. In this way, the generation and implementation of the strategy, although separate issues, are inseparable processes.

Whether strategies really have the support of key people in the organization is an entirely different concern. In reality, it is often overlooked because the process of implementation is, by its very nature, political. Political interactions do occur, largely due to the various differences and friction in any organization. Potential conflict between particular individual's beliefs, values and attitudes; friction between departments; and a lack of understanding between superiors and subordinates is commonplace.

As a result, certain people in the organization may agree with the strategies in theory but consider them impractical to implement. Others may not support the new strategies as they hold a vested interest in maintaining the status quo. Others may find it difficult to identify with one or more of the people who generated the strategies and so provide opposition on more personal grounds. In addition, some people may feel that there is a covert reason why a particular strategy has been generated. Although the strategy itself could seem reasonable, the grounds for its proposal may induce a feeling of mistrust. The end result could be little or no support for, or even opposition to, the proposed strategies.

The machinations surrounding strategy were brought home to us when we came across a European pharmaceutical company which wanted to establish a uniform pricing structure for its product range across Europe. The challenge was Eastern Europe, where market prices naturally reflected local market rates. Entrepreneurial middlemen bought stock from Eastern Europe, often under dummy company names registered in the locality. These products were then sold throughout the rest of Europe at marginally below the market rate but at substantial profit. The CEO brought his GMs together, knowing their opposition to uniform pricing. Each had to achieve their targets – and this was something which uniform pricing would undermine.

The CEO argued the case, stressing the importance of a stable share price and the reputation of the company. He also noted that the current practice was unsustainable, as it left the company vulnerable to takeover. All of this was persuasively logical and undeniably true, but, despite this, opposition to pricing reform continued. 'The case for uniform pricing is that we need one logic for this company. However, where do your loyalties lie, with the centre and the whole business, or just your bits of the company? If you were in my shoes, what would you do? We have a responsibility not only to our shareholders but also to our own people and to our clients and customers. We are the leaders of this company. It is our joint responsibility to provide for a stable future! To do so, each one of us must make a sacrifice', said the CEO to the GMs.

The logic of loyalty to the company, the sacrifice that was necessary and a uniform approach across the markets won the day.

It is important to recognize that the implementation of strategy involves overt and sometimes covert behaviour – at times sharing one's intentions, and at other times not revealing one's true objectives. If the prevailing logic is faulty, the degree of covert behaviour increases considerably.

Once plans for the future have been made, and after pilot projects have been introduced and corrections made to the fundamental strategy, people must be allowed to catch up. Individuals, especially those in key operational positions, have to be given time to identify with the new strategies. People have to become accustomed to new ways of doing things. Training requires time. A multitude of staff and middle management may need to develop different on-the-job skills. Most of all, people need to become involved in implementing any new strategy so that they become committed to making it work. The more substantial the changes, the greater the amount of time people require to identify with, and work towards, the effective implementation of strategy. Yet all of this would not be possible without a compelling argument drawing out the fundamentals of the call for change.

Strategy has to account for projected external influences, such as company image, sources and availability of funds; consumer habits; market trends; material costs; pricing and the availability of energy sources; legislation; and international politics. Strategy which has been clearly thought through acts as a unifying process, clarifying what is and is not feasible in any given situation. Perhaps one reason why so few organizations realize such a level of strategic accomplishment can be put down to the lack of brain power directed at the problem. Strategy developed and executed with IQ is a powerful force.

Structure and IQ

The IQ required to put forward a convincing case for an organization's strategy and how contrasting demands can be synthesized is the first consideration. How to structure the organization so that strategy can be effectively executed is the second.

Every organization operates under some sort of structure. Customers or clients dealing with an organization encounter structure when they select goods to buy, or request a service to meet their needs. They may be seen by one organizational employee, then referred to a second who is thought to better satisfy their needs, and possibly charged for service by a third.

What is important to the organization is that its structure should enable it to harness resources to meet goals. Additionally, the structure needs to have a positive impact on the attitudes and performance of the people in the organization. Structure has to add value.

Inevitably, structures mean a hierarchy of roles. One delivers a service to the public, is quality-managed by the boss, who in turn has a boss, who in turn reports to whoever is running the organization. The application and maintenance of a particular role hierarchy will induce specific views, feelings and attitudes among the people employed by the organization.

A tall hierarchy with limited spans of managerial control will stimulate a formal, controlling leadership style among managers in their relationship with their subordinates. Many employees may feel that the degree of challenge and responsibility in most jobs is limited, for people only need to do what is required of them. Yet, for those who find such a culture acceptable, the degree of identity with the organization is likely to be high. People follow the existing rules and systems, and may genuinely direct their loyalty to the organization rather than to their group or to individuals. The question is, what is the logic of the structure and how does this suit the strategy adopted?

If structure is so important, what is surprising is how few managers can readily identify the range of structures available to them. So let's pose a question: 'How many structural forms exist?' What are the structural possibilities? The consultancy company established just after the Second World War, Urwick Orr, became the structural specialists of their day and, in Europe at least, challenged the predominance of McKinsey. Urwick Orr identified four structural alternatives: functional, product, divisional and matrix.

In a functional structure, all key functions – marketing, sales, production, human resources – are grouped into separate departments, and each of these functions is represented at the strategic decision-making levels. The functions run the business.

A product-structured organization positions outputs – products or services – as the prime focus. This means that each major product line forms a branch of the organizational tree hierarchy, with a director or GM at its head. Each branch features all of the major functional services to support that product line. A duplication of functional services is likely to occur, which increases costs.

A divisional structure involves splitting the organization into separate units, where each one provides a total service to clients according to its purpose, mission and product or service range. Each division is headed by a director, or managing director, and underneath each division a functional, product or matrix structure is adopted. Everything depends on purpose. A divisional structure is most suited for larger organizations.

A matrix structure is a means of integrating support and line functions in such a way that task activity and market responsiveness become one. Or at least this is the theory. Matrix structures were popularized by the National Aeronautics and Space Administration as the best way to have a number of different agencies and companies come together to provide an integrated, seamless service to getting a man on the moon. The concept of straight and direct line relationships (to whom you report and with whom you need to consult) were considered the way to organize for complexity in large, diverse entities.

The reality is somewhat different, however – and can make landing a man on the moon appear straightforward! In practice a matrix manner of operation is more concerned with the attitudes of middle and senior management towards the organization and its purpose. If senior and middle management do not wish to manage their work and interrelationships in a more flexible problem-responsive way, but are more role- and status oriented, then a matrix structure will falter and unwelcome political behaviour result.

Clear delineation of structures is a phenomenon of the past. Very few organizations are principally functional or product structured, unless they are small and not too complex. An exception would be Rolls Royce Aero Engines where focus is on the capability to deliver high-quality engines to the market. In reality, most entities, even in government and the third sector, are a mix of divisional and matrix structures, supported by functional and product substructures.

Structuring organizations is a particularly demanding task. It is one that can make or break any senior manager's career. How many managers have attended meetings outlining the future of the organization and how it should be structured? For the staff and management, an air of trepidation cloaks the room. Restructuring means role changes and possible job losses. Restructuring equals uncertainty and virtually always engenders a combination of fear and scepticism.

Structural design is one of the more demanding IQ challenges faced by organizational leaders. Broad design and minute detail have to be thought through. The litmus test is the reaction of middle management who are tasked with operationalizing the structure whilst still meeting their targets. Clarity of vision and detailed insight concerning implementation are the requirements for structural innovation. No wonder so many careers have derailed due to a lack, or perceived lack, of thinking on what a structure can do.

There is still a third element. Appropriate structural design needs to be accompanied by attention to the information systems that bind together the various elements of the organization.

IQ and information systems

Strategy and structure present formidable intellectual and practical challenges. There is more, much more. For any organization to succeed, it has to ensure that the activities of its units, departments and divisions are well coordinated through the development and use of a management information system (MIS). MIS is the key determinant of organization structure, especially as its prime aim is to improve the quality of decision-making, problem-solving, the rapid transmission of information concerning customers and the accurate capturing of financial information.

A well-thought-through MIS is the linking mechanism of the organization, especially in the diverse and complex organizations of our times. But, get it right and the potential pay-offs are enormous:

1. **Improved long-term planning.** In a private-sector organization, the data for long-term planning becomes more accessible. Sales data, for example, can be broken down by each geographic area, or time taken for a range of products to be sold. In public service organizations the data required for future planning can be more difficult to define, but even in the field of social work brave attempts have been made to develop systematic recording and review systems, providing important information on social worker activities. This detail can be easily utilized by senior managers for long-term planning.

2. **Enhanced managerial control.** The speed of provision of information is as important as its accuracy. A major problem for any organization is that information needed quickly by management is not rapidly forthcoming from those operating lower down in the organization. An efficient MIS provides management with the detail it needs and will also be seen by

those lower in the hierarchy as useful rather than yet another interference.

3. **Reduced conflict.** An information system that binds disinterested parties to each other is likely to reduce the potential level of aggravation between groups. First, all interested parties will know what is required of them and why. Second, individuals can plan their workload because they know what type of information they have to gather and refer upwards. A nagging frustration for many at work is that people at all levels in the hierarchy may be asked to provide or find information without any prior warning. Worse still is continuously responding to demands for information that most feel is irrelevant and time wasting to compile. Sometimes they do not know where to begin to search or why the information is needed. Working according to a common, meaningful information system will reduce levels of frustration.

4. **Improved motivation.** People who know what is expected of them can plan for future events and know that what they are doing is purposeful. They are motivated to work within specified boundaries where they are more certain of their position. The more people know what is required of them, the less need for continuous supervisory attention.

In a small organization, employing a small number of people, there is less need to arrange people's roles and relationships formally. Individuals will conduct their business with each other face-to-face, especially the allocation of task responsibilities. Equally, the process of quality control is personalized as individuals are likely to praise or criticize one another's performance as the occasion arises.

As we have discussed, managers find themselves continually utilizing high IQ to redesign the structure of their group, section, department, division or organization. Organizational charts may be drafted and redrafted, while individual areas of responsibility and authority are often redefined and budgets for additional personnel and equipment are usually under constant scrutiny. In this way, managers in the organization are able to argue for the continued development of their establishment. The arguments and points of view may be many and varied, and at times in direct contradiction to each other. Nevertheless, some form of cohesion needs to emerge.

In effect, organizational structure needs to be viewed as a means to an end. Structure provides the fundamental means by which key strategies and objectives are pursued. As one prime purpose of structure is to act as a vehicle of implementation of organization strategy, it is vital that any analysis encompass a broad brief.

It is a waste of time, money and energy to generate strategy that is simply inoperable within the existing structure of the organization and yet is implemented without any accompanying structural change. However, if changes of structure are contemplated, then it is necessary to assess the likely success of change realistically. Successful structural change involves an analysis beyond the narrow confines of role hierarchy.

IQ and sourcing

A further and more recent structural component is outsourcing. Why do everything in-house when particular activities can be contracted out to specialists? Although outsourcing has been given a great deal of attention, it is only one component of sourcing. Activities can be sourced out as well as back in, and both are in keeping with the strategy being pursued, thus the term 'smart sourcing'. The smart executive is one who knows when to source in or out and then is able to act on that judgement.

Smart sourcing is another IQ challenge. What is being sourced in or out this year may not be the same next year. This is now an important component of competitive advantage. A critical benefit of outsourcing is cost reduction. Pursuing outsourcing for purposes of economies of scale can also increase internal efficiencies. Research shows that outsourcing can strategically change an organization, assisting management in analysing the extent to which the firm is differentiated from its competitors and therefore emerging with a clear value identity for the enterprise.

As a result, resources are repositioned to be more focused on achieving particular goals and targets.

Differentiating the enterprise from the competition is becoming ever more necessary as consumers and shareholders will switch their attention and loyalties elsewhere if, in their eyes, value for money is not being delivered. It is the appropriate positioning or sourcing of resources that provides the enterprise with the leverage it needs to meet consumer demands in terms of quality and price, and to satisfy shareholder requirements for continued profitability and growth.

It is worth noting that outsourcing is not a new phenomenon. The Romans contracted out tax collection. In the eighteenth and nineteenth centuries, England's public services benefitted from the private sector in the form of street lighting, prison management, road maintenance, the collection of taxes, refuse collection and other public revenues under contract to local authorities. During the same period, similar arrangements existed in America and Australia, where private operations provided mail delivery, and in France the construction and management of the railway network and other distribution facilities was contracted out to commercial companies through competitive tendering.

Matters changed with the onset of the twentieth century. Volume-based production encouraged the large, vertically integrated enterprise, as opposed to the myriad of smaller organizations providing contractually based services on behalf of government. Such developments reversed the trend towards 'contracting out'.

Ironically, the very same factors that led to a retreat from contracting out have fostered its resurgence over the past fifteen years. It is no longer cost effective to maintain specialist services in-house. Greater professional and economic benefit is gained by releasing such resources into the marketplace to fend for themselves. On this basis, external providers are now offered the opportunity to deliver services on a scale that many single organizations would find it difficult to match.

Accompanying these changes of organizational form has been a change of mindset, from management to leadership. The perception that relative power within organizations is symbolized by the size of budget and the number of employees within a manager's domain has been replaced by concern with concepts, such as profitability, service, cost control and value enhancement. Managers are more focused on running lean organizations than large empires. Managing internal organizational processes is giving way to achieving targets and demonstrating value.

The impact of outsourcing on the host organization varies from one enterprise to the next, from identifying and applying tactical solutions to practical problems, such as contracting out routine ancillary services, through to clarifying the strategic direction that needs to be pursued by the organization. To integrate this variety of initiatives, from the tactical to the strategic, and in ways that meet the needs of the host enterprise, while being contextually sensitive and economically valid, requires high IQ and as previously mentioned, smart decision-making.

A smart company anticipates the challenges associated with the out or in of the sourcing of its activities and actively minimizes the discomfort to its employees. Experience suggests that it is impossible to avoid some dip in employee morale when a company makes an outsourcing announcement, but it is possible to avoid long-term negative effects. So much is dependent on both the HR arrangements which can make or break an outsourcing initiative and the board's involvement in the sourcing exercise. Research shows that most boards are not in touch with what is being sourced in and out of their organization, and so do not ask relevant questions about these important components of competitive advantage. This sourcing, which could provide distinct competitive advantage, all too often is treated as an operational rather than a strategic lever.

In contrast, successful private- and public-sector enterprises smartly source their enterprises in ways which secure economics of scale, while also providing improvements in quality of service. This is done through a dynamic, performance-oriented partnership with suppliers in different competitive networks to achieve optimum results. Smart sourcing involves managing an array of sourcing contracts and arrangements that helps the enterprise concentrate on achieving its strategic and operational goals.

Governance and IQ

Strategy, structure, information systems and sourcing provide sizeable challenges. Understanding them and implementing them successfully requires IQ of the highest order. The final IQ frontier for leaders in organizations of all sorts is governance.

Governance penetrates a wide variety of aspects of our life. How we should conduct ourselves on a train, in a taxi, in a park, in a shop and at a restaurant is clearly visible on the signs saying, 'Do not smoke', 'Do not walk on the grass', 'Be respectful to other customers' and 'Be quiet in the quiet carriage on the train.' In effect, governance is both a set of protocols which shape desirable behaviour and the oversight to ensure those protocols are adhered to and respected.

This is true nowhere more so than in the corporation, government agency or non-governmental organization (NGO). The guardian of governance is the board, composed of mainly non-executive (part-time directors), who may also have on the board the CEO and the finance director/chief financial officer (CFO) The duties bestowed on boards are increasing. Board directors hold the same legal exposure and accountability as executive directors, the full-timers. So they are held responsible for all aspects of the organization's functioning, strategy determination and execution, risk assessment and defence of reputation.

In theory, the influence of the board is all pervasive. In practice, boards are repeatedly accused of not providing value. Why? For many reasons, one being because many non-executive directors (NEDs) hold too many board positions and are therefore unable to devote sufficient time for oversight. The other is that NEDs are often viewed as being out of touch.

Research indicates that three to four board-level positions are the maximum number that any individual can successfully embrace while dealing with the important, and often hidden, challenges organizations face. In practice, far more appointments may be held. For example, the most recent statistics indicate that thirteen concurrently held directorships in the United States and fourteen in South Africa are not uncommon. The routine of many of these overloaded non-executives is to attend board meetings (in reality treated as committee meetings), look at the papers in front of them, debate, make some decisions and then walk away. No wonder the conclusion is that board directors can so easily be out of touch with the company. Decisions can be made in a bubble.

Australian, and more recently FTSE100 companies, are the exception, where NEDs who hold a portfolio of more than three or four directorships are pressured to drop additional directorships before joining a new board.

As governance today is so encroaching, considerable thought needs to be given to scrutinizing the strategy, structural design and its effects, in order to realize competitive advantage and ensure the viability of the company. Good governance accurately determines risks, defends reputation and creates the groundwork for sustainability. Yet, in our survey of UK boards (from FTSE100 to 350), managers admitted to gaining little value from their board. The most common criticisms were not thinking about what will work and not giving sufficient attention to learn about the organization.

Thanks to the complexities involved, it is virtually impossible for any NED to fully understand the details of what is happening throughout the organization. Irrespective of this, demand for corporate governance and decision-making transparency is increasing. Boards have become easy targets for the power they wield and their real or imagined impacts upon entire economies.

The result of this is that chairmen and NEDs are becoming – quite rightly – concerned about their professional and legal liabilities as well as their moral responsibilities. Their risk-taking appetite is progressively reducing by the likelihood of them making serious mistakes which could result in the redundancies of thousands of people or even the failure of an organization.

This is pushing some boards towards supporting CEOs without necessarily addressing or acting upon their experience or instinct about the information placed in front of them. Also, due to a lack of insight about how the organization really operates, board members find it difficult to challenge the data put to them by management. The lack of time to gain the necessary insights inhibits NEDs from challenging their counterparts on core issues.

The number one question for both aspiring and existing board members is, 'Do they really understand their organization's competitive advantage and how it should be positioned?' Careful consideration should be given to how board members interpret and deliver governance which enables a business to perform more effectively, while maintaining grounded ethical and moral positions in the marketplace.

For example, what is the financial exposure and risk to reputation with a prospective acquisition? Are more malleable targets available? With a comprehensive merger or acquisition, will shareholder value be damaged when promising substantial gain?

Due to pressures of time or a reluctance to be held accountable, the key IQ-reliant mentoring influences that should be on offer from a boardroom – support, stewardship and leadership – are becoming increasingly negligent in this respect. A consequence of this lack of accountability means that it is managers, rather than board directors, who face blame when things go wrong.

Moving forward

So what can be done to address these seemingly insurmountable challenges, and how should boards go forward to achieve their organizational purpose?

More than anything else, NEDs need to be clear about their own purpose. If they are to genuinely add value to an organization, they must understand that engaging with management teams and workforces is vital, and can only be achieved through an ongoing and honest dialogue with a multitude of stakeholders. This requires serious consideration of their role and whether they are capable of making a meaningful contribution to each board on which they sit. Each board needs to be treated as unique in order for a NED to shape purpose and deliver real value.

Central to this is the chairperson. In order for the board to make meaningful contributions, the chairperson needs to consider

- setting the ethical tone for the board and the company;

- identifying and participating in selecting board members and overseeing a succession plan for the board;

- identifying and selecting the CEO and overseeing a succession plan for all senior management positions;

- formulating the yearly work plan for the board, CEO and certain senior managers;

- managing conflicts of interest;

- ensuring that directors play a full and constructive role in the affairs of the company;

- monitoring how the board works together;

- mentoring and stewarding the management through challenges;

- ensuring good relations are maintained with the company's major shareholders and strategic stakeholders;

- evaluating the future of the company and what is in the best interest of the stakeholders, employees and customers/clients;

- analysing to go about defence of reputation; and

- assessing and minimizing risk.

This list is not exhaustive but becomes particularly relevant when held up against our research with leading Financial Times Stock Exchange (FTSE) companies, which identifies many boards as being significantly disengaged from their companies and struggling to respond to rapid market changes. This point is brought home by our surveys that showed that over 80 per cent of board members simply do not know or have no shared view concerning the competitive advantage of their firm.

Ultimately, boards have to deal with unique sets of circumstances no matter how much procedural governance is put in place. However, they effect positive change by attending to board succession and the recruitment of NEDs. The selection criteria for non-executives is consistently unclear, and boards must rid themselves of a debilitating 'clubbiness' in making new appointments. One senor headhunter admitted to us, privately, that 80 per cent of appointments to boards in the City of London are predetermined by the chairperson and/or the CEO. In New York, it is 90 per cent.

All-round IQ

Ultimately, IQ is the single component of the 5Qs which is consistent with whichever job you may have and at whatever level of management.

The argument for employing IQ in the face of complexity is very simple and repeated throughout this chapter: competitive advantage. In the private sector, reaching a shared view on competitive advantage is critical. In NGOs and the public sector the prime consideration is value delivery, namely meeting citizen/community needs. The end point for both public and private sectors is the value delivered and to whom.

Competitive advantage has traditionally been defined from the top down and can be witnessed where the board may run into repeated problems or creep to a standstill because the general and middle management have to implement a detached and untested strategy.

Smarter organizations work things the opposite way around by building their model of competitive advantage from the bottom up. So, for a motor manufacturer operating globally, the reality is that a competitive advantage in China will prove to be a very different experience in Europe. In China, the competitive advantage may result from strong government relations and a subsequent ability to influence policy and handle regulation. In Europe, it may be the high standards of customer service and positive relationships with after-sale service centres. Different views on competitive advantage can happily coexist, but it takes IQ to effectively align these interests and create a model which takes into account market pressures and social and political circumstances.

To achieve this, it is necessary to develop a model that makes sense of competitive advantage and then test it through others so that through their participation all can believe in it, particularly as everyone's job includes customer service. Building on service internally enables employees to practice this philosophy externally. The ability to translate competitive advantage into action and break it into components is a broad, complex, smart and evidence-based process.

IQ functions at different levels. As mentioned previously, boards and top teams are a meeting point of different agendas and interests, with the board being more concerned with governance, and the top team with strategy creation and execution. General management teams are subsequently caught between the negotiation of interests and the achievement of tasks and objectives, which are the function of operational teams.

In order to realize competitive advantage, governance protocols and oversight through stewardship must be positioned so as to add value to the organization rather than hinder it. In the first instance a debate has to take place between the CEO and the chairperson to establish how value will be delivered externally. This is followed by a conversation to define the boundaries between the board and the management team, and how the two should operate. In this way clarity concerning how both will add value to their organization is clear and appreciated.

In practise, how many organizations really operate like this across the world? According to our studies, no more than 18–20 per cent. Most instead choose to run with the traditional approach of 'this is my role as chairperson, this is my role as CEO, this is the board, this is the top team'. This does not deliver much in the way of value.

For that 18–20 per cent, the questions asked are 'Why do this?' or 'Why not look at how we differentiate boundaries according to strategic market challenges?' The debate on how to deliver value starts. For the remainder, the response may be 'I never thought of it', or 'My job as chairperson is this, you fix it', or 'I'm CEO, you don't touch it.' What is often demonstrated is that there is plenty of emotion at play, while IQ is sadly lacking. It is a genuine problem if you are unable to stand back from your role and analyse the value you deliver, which should be to create a unique view of competitive advantage. If, as CEO or chairperson you haven't done this, challenging circumstances will often get in the way of IQ and illicit an emotional reaction rather than a considered viewpoint drawing on IQ.

After reaching agreement on the competitive advantage of the organization, the second issue to address is how to get value out of individual roles, whether this relates to the chairperson, CEO, board or top team. The different responsibilities and accountabilities that need to be built into these roles are important because they lead to a debate about the exercise of realizing competitive advantage and who owns the strategy. This does away with the time-consuming and unproductive 'I do/no, I do' back and forth which can emerge.

Whoever owns the strategy is the person who has to live with it and recreate it on a daily basis. Research emphasizes this is the CEO and top team. Some chairpersons and boards argue that they must own the strategy in order to act if something goes seriously wrong. But how can you be responsible for strategy when you attend a board meeting just once a month, or are present at subcommittee meetings, or come to the company two days a week? If something is wrong, it is not necessarily with the strategy. The board's role is to analyse problems with the person who owns that strategy and is responsible for the management team. Most problems are not simply strategy related. Strategies are often quite reasonable, which means it is a person who has a lack of understanding of situational reality. When things go wrong it's usually due to poor execution. IQ becomes even more important when people don't engage but management disregards this resistance and continues to push forward regardless.

Again our research shows that best practice is that management owns the strategy, but the board owns the culture. The board's responsibility is to understand and guide through the fault lines and pitfalls that occur during the process of strategy implementation. Now management can do its job effectively. This makes the board act as steward, which leads to questions of how they can best negotiate with management and make contact with lower-level management without undermining the top team.

How do you penetrate culture as a board and tackle organizational fault lines, which everyone recognizes but nobody dares do anything about? This is a fundamental IQ challenge. How many boards have actually considered that they own culture and questioned what to do with responsibility, as opposed to fighting management over who owns strategy or just giving in to management and ticking off on it?

Boards exist to protect organizations by overseeing and safeguarding their interests. This means they have to strike a balance between monitoring and adopting the control procedures and protocols which display high stands of governance and stewardship, which is the guiding and coaching through uncomfortable concerns and paradoxes as they really happen on the ground.

The word 'stewardship' means being able to delve deeply into the organization and facilitate the delivery of objectives. Monitoring without stewardship means inadequate, unproductive governance.

Soft going

Robert Swannel, chairman of Marks and Spencer, an investment banker with no background in retail, has proved integral along with the CEO in turning around the global repositioning of this firm. How has he, as chairman of the board, added value? He has tasked his NEDs to be members of 'seminar groups' composed of middle managers and staff of Marks and Spencer. Meeting regularly, discussions can be broad, but the NEDs can now bring the insights of their deliberations about crucial topics to the board and address the fault lines. In partnership with management, NED Swannel is balancing stewardship with monitoring. It will be interesting to see how this initiative works out.

Dealing with the fault lines, enhancing engagement with stakeholders, defending reputation and instigating a culture of service is in essence about pursuing soft strategy. One key element of the soft side of strategy is corporate social responsibility (CSR), which sees human rights and transparency prioritized alongside product promotion and an emphasis on quality service. Some board directors are now given a portfolio of responsibilities to specifically identify the CSR problems the organization and its supply chains face. Taking this information to the board; entering into discussion about what can be done and laying the ground for, at times, an uncomfortable conversation, rather than ignoring difficult and seemingly impossible situations altogether, is all about IQ. What is the compelling argument that encourages people to listen when they do not wish to?

Despite many CEOs and chairmen not wishing to enter into this debate, the responsibilities of the corporation are now open to scrutiny. How CSR or CR (corporate responsibility) are integrated with corporate strategy is critical. A discerning press and public now demand greater accountability from the company, not only in terms of its profitability but also its exercise of responsibility to the broader community. Attempting change will not fall into any of the other Qs without IQ, and if something is going to fail, the first place it will do so is in the argument.

If the true sense of purpose and mission is to provide a service to customers both fairly and honourably, then change has to happen. The GM cannot change the reality of how the organization operates. They can only execute a strategy but cannot change the fundamental design of the place.

This process asks how an organization should be designed so that it is fit for purpose. Organization redesign cannot escape engaging vital IQ qualities, such as addressing prime purpose as well as moral and ethical values. Most organizations have a series of value, mission and vision statements, which are counterproductive and meaningless because people do not believe in them when they witness the reality of how their workplace actually operates.

To avoid such high levels of demotivation, IQ must be employed to establish either a mission- or a vision-based organization. There are important and notable differences between the two, as our research in the recent book *The Success Formula* highlights.

A mission-based organization lives by deeply established values that ensure that value in the other sense is delivered. Vision-based organizations are often the outcome of the aspirations of the CEO, with or without the top team, and are based on a value proposition – a vision of how value might be delivered in the future.

The vision approach has been witnessed in many ways with the Manchester United Football Club, which is an admirable money-generating Goliath, combining shareholder value and football accomplishment. By the time its legendary manager, Sir Alex Ferguson, left the club, he had created a very distinct set of values regarding professionalism, football and the training of home-grown players and the selective purchase of high-priced players. After he had gone, this ethos changed, which suggests these values were never fully embedded. On consideration, could the club have done more to embed the values that Ferguson so prominently lived and promoted? Without this, the club's strategy becomes one of finding a new messiah to reconnect them with their own past.

Organizational design means determining the prime purpose, whether this is mission- or vision led. Tough questions need to be asked, such as 'Why are things being done in this particular way?' and

'Are our current values really being lived?' The next action to take is a decision on what sort of structure to create.

Organizational design is based on modelling, evidence, capabilities and an assessment of those capabilities. IQ should be high at these levels, but when not exercised this has consequences, often in the form of restructures that go wrong. Mission statements that don't capture reality or how people live, lead to a rejection of core values so that nothing binds an organization together. If vision is driven by a factor that nobody can engage with, everything then becomes tactical and the organization is vulnerable to scandal or changing circumstances in the market.

In such a situation, general management becomes caught between having a very clear view on strategy, because they are living it on a day-to-day basis, and being responsible for executing a plan they have no responsibility for or involvement in creating. On top of this, they know if it won't work, even before it is attempted. General management has to use IQ to analyse and anticipate the consequences of their actions. They balance giving critical feedback up the chain as much as they can, while at the same time trying to harness the motivation of the people working below them.

When employees ask, 'Why is my general manager doing something they know won't work?' they begin to lose trust in the process. Managing this complexity needs to be carefully thought through. Questions to review include 'How am I going to handle this?', 'How am I going to position messages?', 'How am I going to deliver messages upwards?' and 'How long will it take before the real message gets through?' All of these important IQ challenges are central to being able to win colleagues over and talk to them openly, without being disloyal to the organizational objectives and directives from above.

Below general management, IQ is far less strategic but more concerned with role, task and function. A surgeon is a highly intelligent person, but they are not paid to work out ward schedules or how the hospital runs. They are there to consult, operate and do their job. This is where IQ can be at its very best, when individuals have some insight into the organization's disparities, tensions and paradoxes alongside the delivery of their job. Yet many people are not able to distance themselves sufficiently and opt to rebel or rage against an unsatisfactory job because they do not possess organizational insight, nor are they required to. Their complexity is functional based.

To possess a mindset of functionality at the senior level can have damaging, unwelcome consequences. The board's and top team's question is, 'Why have we positioned resources in the way we have when greater value could be achieved through a more fruitful repositioning'? The general management resource and strategy question is, 'What's happening to loyalty?' If decisions keep shifting, loyalty will get damaged and this is what binds them together. So two levels of leadership are looking at repositioning from different perspectives. One is looking for continuity and the other is seeking a future possibly beyond this current organization. No wonder people of high IQ clash. Each logic on its own may be impeccable, but together?

IQ is the overriding basis for developing a compelling argument for the allocation of resources and the positioning of assets to realize competitive advantage and deliver value. Clear, comprehensive strategy is the link between mission statements and the effective implementation of particular tasks – the vital connection between the desired and the attainable.

A high IQ is fundamental to outstanding leadership, although evidence suggests that highly successful people with high IQs sometimes fail when promoted into leadership roles. But if you don't do IQ, forget the rest.

One CEO interviewed stated that he spends 40 per cent of his time running the business, and the other 60 per cent trying to understand how the people and organization 'tick'. This indicates that other forms of intelligence also determine leadership ability.

Action points

The following questions are intended to help you consider how you use intellect (IQ) in your organization and leadership role.

- How will you position your resources to deliver value?

- What sorts of structures are you going to introduce to support value creation?

- Why will you use those structures rather than other structures?

- How does the structure fit with your strategy?

- Utimately, with IQ, the purpose is to come up with a compelling argument for the value creation strategy. What is your compelling argument?

2

EQ: Harnessing emotions, enhancing relationships

Elvira had just taken over a major division of the company. Her predecessor was charismatic but also chaotic, giving favour to those she liked and neglecting all others. The divisional team had coped by meeting with Elvira's predecessor one-to-one. Irrespective of what was agreed at meetings, decisions would be turned around depending on who influenced the predecessor the most. Certain individuals benefited from this form of political interaction. But, any notion of teamwork was absent. When Elvira took over the leadership reins that was what worried her most. At her first meeting with the team Elvira spelt out the ground rules:

- What we agree at meetings we stick to.
- There will be no seeing me after the meeting to get your way.
- There will be no seeing me before the meeting to get your way.

- There will be no seeing my boss to get your way (that had also been a common practice).

- The budget will be transparent to all.

- Performance and bonuses will also be transparent to all.

Most in the team took a sharp breath. They were unaccustomed to such plain talking. 'I understand that this may be difficult for some of you, but let me work with you and talk things through with you so that we really become a good team', said Elvira.

Over the next few months, Elvira worked closely with the team and with the individuals who needed more of her attention. She spoke openly and sincerely about the strengths and weaknesses of the organization and the team, allowing her colleagues to respond in similar fashion.

A new way of behaving slowly surfaced. The team's concerns, problems, ideas and accomplishments were openly discussed and colleagues positively challenged. The new 'va va voom' spurred a cutting edge to doing business combined with sensitive support of each other. In the winning of contracts, personal and organizational interests were put aside, and that most clearly showed in the servicing of clients. Even Elvira's boss, a subtle political operator, commented, 'It's refreshing to see your new style and what you are doing with your team. It may even catch on with the rest of the organization.'

Elvira smiled. 'That would be a first for this place', she thought.

Smooth operators

Emotional quotient, or EQ, is the ability to manage your own emotions and the emotions of others. EQ offers another way of looking at relationships, especially those which need continuous attention to remain aligned. Over time, EQ has evolved into the ability to accurately perceive emotions, improve thought processes and, in so doing, reflectively regulate and promote intellectual growth. In effect, being attentive to EQ distinctly enables a higher and continued level of chemistry between individuals.

While our research has established that IQ is by far the most important of the 5Qs in terms of how conflicting data is used to construct compelling arguments, EQ is a way to smooth relationships which may be challenged as a result of a powerful advocacy.

Research shows that people with high EQ have better mental health and greater job performance, and display more accomplished leadership skills. Daniel Goleman, the popularizer of emotional intelligence, has indicated that EQ accounts for up to 67 per cent of the abilities deemed necessary for superior performance in leaders, and matters twice as much as technical expertise or IQ.

In any organization of between 70 and 1,000 people or more, a lack of effective EQ can result in high levels of misalignment between intentions, agendas and actions. Where differences should be at a minimum, continued tension and strife can become overwhelming because of a lack of focus on EQ. Life is much better when we are all more EQ accomplished.

What are the EQ qualities a great leader requires?

1. Self-awareness – the ability to know one's emotions, strengths, weaknesses, drives, values and goals; being able to recognize one's impact on others and, through such insight, to use gut feelings to guide decisions

2. Self-regulation – controlling or redirecting one's disruptive emotions and impulses, and adapting to changing circumstances

3. Social skill – managing relationships to move people in a mutually desired direction

4. Empathy – considering other people's feelings, especially when making decisions

5. Motivation – being driven to achieve for the sake of achievement

6. Moral core – working towards treating others equally and in a transparent manner

As EQ is about managing one's own emotions and the emotions of others, it is ideally suited as a way of sharing team concerns, building relations and enhancing performance. EQ works best where relatively clear goals, mission and purpose underpin the team. In effect, the critical challenge is to enhance engagement, particularly where interests and agendas are misaligned. Where tension undermines engagement and damages alignment of thinking and interests, pursuing an EQ approach is unlikely to lead to positive results. In this instance being PQ oriented is required (the topic of our next chapter).

In many ways EQ began as a counteraction to excessive focus on the practice and pursuit of competitive advantage to the point where nothing else matters. To counter such excessive zeal, EQ emphasizes four types of abilities:

1. Perceiving emotions in faces, images, voices, body language and actions, including the ability to identify one's

own emotions. This makes the processing of emotional information possible.

2. Using emotions to think through issues and problem-solve. An EQ approach allows an individual to benefit from changing moods to tackle a particular task.

3. Comprehending emotions allows for a better appreciation of complex sensitivities which evolve over time.

4. Better managing emotions in both oneself and others, enables the shaping emotions to achieve mutually desired goals.

In the 1950s, 1960s and 1970s, markets were buoyant and the notion of EQ (not known as such then) was considered a luxury. Yes, it would be nice to treat people well, but did it really make any difference? Once markets matured and became saturated, the concept of EQ and the importance of personal relationships came to the fore. It became clearer that being pleasant, understanding and patient enabled teams to pull together and stimulate transparency, which naturally improved service.

This matters because transparency is naturally linked to authenticity and consistency, which are qualities that those in senior positions often struggle to maintain. The EQ concept searches for deep connections between individuals and teams, but relationships differ with each scenario, depending on who shapes the direction an organization should take. Friendships may remain, but at a certain level the notion of 'what needs to be done and how' takes over. This is the division between the objective and personal sides of PQ and EQ. (Such differences will be explained in the next chapter.)

An established view is that some people are characteristically more EQ oriented than others, and there is some evidence to support this claim. Our research has discovered a limited number of males and females who have scored zero on feelings in psychometric tests such as the Myers Briggs. This means they are low on emotional awareness and demonstrate high dependence on logical arguments. This isn't to say that such individuals do not experience emotions. They do. But it is more that emotions, as a way of working, do not enter their mindset. They could be drawn towards logic, drive or even aggression, but their ability to read context and people is minimal.

EQ has often been recognized as more of a female characteristic, and yet our database has recorded a considerable number of female senior executives who have '0 feelings' scores. This may be due to continued experience, even from childhood, of using logic and deduction as a way of living. In the nature of these individuals relationships have always taken second place. This may also be because, to do well in some roles, EQ qualities are viewed as being surplus to requirements. (It is also of note that we are witnessing an era with the highest number of female executives being taken to tribunal for bullying and harassment claims, with their accusers predominantly being women.)

So, if you are not gifted with EQ as a trait, then the only other option is to develop the skills involved. This journey includes learning to appreciate and draw upon the power of context, handle resentment and know how to give and receive feedback.

The power of context

When it comes to learning EQ, ironically the first step is not to pay attention to reading people but instead to focus on their context. This translates into a process of surveying a new organization and meeting with people who may be nice, unpleasant or otherwise, and then beginning to learn what their situation is actually like.

In these circumstances, always ask yourself the question, 'What is driving particular patterns of behaviour or predominant ways of thinking?' It is from this point that it becomes possible to start developing a framework to help examine the specifics of a situation.

To understand the context, ask the following questions:

- What is the nature of the culture in the organization?

- What makes sense to people inside, but does not to those outside?

- To what extent do managers reflect on their actions and reactions?

- To what extent do managers assume that what they do and think is normal?

- How are challenges dealt with – positively, defensively, transparently or covertly?

- Who are the heroes of the organization – past and present – and why are they revered?

- How would you know that you have stepped beyond the mark of acceptable behaviour?

- Is feedback offered openly? Is everything satisfactory on the surface, or in reality does damaging and unwelcome tension exist in the background?

- How well are newcomers integrated into the culture?

Your responses to these questions will provide clear clues as to the nature and culture of the organization and the EQ challenge that needs to be faced to effectively build positive relationships.

Context can be driven by legacy or by a specific business demand, such as hitting sales targets. Is the context in question aggressive, suffering from short-termism, or just plain pushy? Is the context politically charged by personalities who don't know how to reconcile concerns and best discuss critical issues with others? Is it just one or two personalities shaping the culture? Is it that intrinsically people are decent and respectful of each other, but have not as yet exhibited a different side to them? All of these factors can be highly valued or detrimental, and also serve to undermine or encourage an EQ orientation.

If context is well measured and handled, and people are deeply conscious of what relationships mean and are seeking to get the best out of their colleagues, then a set of operational values emerge. These direct how thinking is processed and the operation is best managed. In other words, context is understood and can be moulded. Leaders adapt to this reality, or are otherwise viewed as weak, out of touch, unduly assertive and unable to see the big picture. Regardless of whether context is overly passive or aggressive, the leader becomes undermined and underappreciated.

Understand the people

The next step is to understand the people around you and observe how they react emotionally. What triggers a positive or negative reaction? What stimulates a good conversation? How do individuals appear to think and feel? The characteristics of context and people can appear almost identical, but the order in which they are viewed and acted upon is important.

In many minds the two elements overlap. As stated, the instinctive approach is first to read people and then to consider the context. This can lead to serious misjudgements. So, instead, begin with context to explain what is actually happening on the ground. Then follow up with observations of individuals to begin creating a clear view of why basic patterns of behaviour are occurring and how certain individuals comply or are difficult. This process requires serious discipline, which follows a specific order:

1. I can see what people do/don't do

2. I can see what people say/don't say

3. I can see how particular people comply/don't comply

4. I recognize what they are doing

5. I recognize what they should be doing

6. I can see how I need to keep quiet in certain situations

7. I know when I need to ask questions

These steps help individuals to relate more effectively to each other and react appropriately. One of the first positive outcomes is the building of trust based on visible patterns of behaviour and authenticity. Yet, with such insight, EQ can still be difficult to put into action. Through no fault of their own, managers may be tasked to drive a 'yes, we can do this this' mentality, while also being required to react consistently and sensitively to people operating in a contradictory context.

Furthermore, what happens if you are a leader who is trying to be authentic, but then circumstances change? Do you simply carry on, knowing that in a new situation the wrong path is being followed? Or, do you pause and deliver an updated assessment and new message as part of an ongoing EQ process?

Irrespective of such pressures and demands, maintaining authenticity has to be addressed. This means there is a requirement when circumstances shift substantially to communicate why previously established intentions have changed. This is achieved by helping others see and understand the context, which allows them to align their perspective and thinking accordingly.

EQ doesn't mean having to think the same way as others, but is more about how to manage your emotions. If we are playing a game of soccer, we have to score goals, and this involves how we pass, defend and attack. How we do this is up to us. How we attack and defend together, how we cover for each other and how we support each other, especially when one member of the team has made an error, can win or lose a game.

Ultimately, the focal point of concern is the person. You need to understand their situation, but at the same time you cannot blame the situation. It is what it is. The need for self-insight and acceptance of feedback and personal development is vital. The ability to handle situations differently is also an important aspect which crosses over into both the EQ and the PQ domain. EQ means that over time you become trusted. You are recognized as behaving authentically most of the time, and are forgiven if this persona ever slips because others can see that your actions are genuine and circumstances are taken into account.

EQ needs a platform through which intentions can be clearly outlined and communicated. It is important to prepare people so that they can listen to and understand new developments designed for their own and the wider organization's benefit. New people coming into a team may need time to adjust to the way people do things – becoming used to people talking more openly, or perhaps appearing more aggressive while still being good friends. This again is part of a longer-term process of appreciating context in order to build trust.

The next step in preparing the communication platform is to build the capability of others to take part. EQ is very important in the positive shaping of personal relationships. If you consider what might happen when you are at home, you instinctively know that you and your partner can enter into a process of communication, but in the workplace you don't always feel able to get involved in a discussion. You may feel unprepared, unready or unwilling to join in. Of course, in dysfunctional home environments, the same situation occurs.

Other people might seem angry or uncooperative. In order to get them to talk, you will have to manage these emotions. This requires patience and time. It may take three or six months to achieve, as you gradually prepare them to discuss challenging circumstances. Even then you might never reach this point. Building the capability of others to listen is vital, and immense sensitivity is required. You are seeing an individual in their context and looking at how far they can be stretched without allowing resentment to creep in. And this is important as resentment is one of the greatest threats to harmonious and cohesive relationships.

Resentment

Resentment is a logic and state of mind that belongs to your own personal history. You may be stretched to achieve 'X, Y and Z', but resent the instigator of this work. Despite seeing that they are technically right, you may not like the way they have spoken to you or raised an issue, or feel that they have inadvertently or directly identified your weaknesses. Resentment is personal. It is totally down to you. Even if this other person can manage their own emotions and is trying to manage yours, you may still resent them. This means there is something from the past that is getting in the way of your discussion in the present.

Resentment emerges when you view someone as negatively impacting upon you. They undermine your interests. They appear to view you as being less able, and try to steer you or push hard in a particular direction. The other person may genuinely try to be supportive, but you don't like the tone or nature of their conversation. Alternatively, your resentment of the person may be entirely justified. Whatever your reasoning, you become focused on feeling that your ideas and contribution are better than those of another person. In fact, you feel you are better off out of the situation, but escape is not always easy. Resentment in people's personal relationships can last a lifetime, and this can also be the case at work. You may have left the organization many years ago, but when you meet your former boss, even though they may seem to have changed, keeping your resentment under control can be demanding.

Individuals can work and live together, but resentment bubbles along just beneath the surface. Resentment can, and does, undermine relationships without entirely killing them, making individuals blind to changes in people and to different circumstances. Resentment can drive a pattern of interaction, even though the original tension has long since disappeared.

In our research we have discovered that people who are more 'feelings oriented' may have a clear EQ mindset, which should in turn enable them to be better equipped to handle resentment than those who are less sensitive. However, this is not always the case. Being hurt penetrates them deeply, and these feelings remain for a long time. In contrast, those who had hardly any score on feelings more often than not express a 'so what?' attitude. While impacted, in terms of their relationships, they cannot comprehend why emotions are allowed to get in the way of the bigger picture. 'Me, I'm more practical and don't let such unproductive feelings get in the way' is a sentiment that is often expressed.

One arena which has been tested in terms of EQ adoption is the British Civil Service. The preoccupation of Anglo American economies with cutting costs in government and having the private sector accept responsibility for delivery of services to the community, has substantially changed the shape of the civil service. In the UK it is quite astounding how well senior civil servants have implemented the severe cuts imposed by the government.

One civil servant faced a substantial reduction to his budget. He was newly appointed and came from a different discipline to that of his department. His immediate reaction was to work together with all relevant parties within his department and accept responsibility for implementing an unpopular and unwelcome financial strategy. He consulted with all relevant internal and external stakeholders and thoroughly mapped out the key areas of concern to policy execution. He identified the fault lines in the organization and then, together with others, established ways to bypass these blockages to the delivery of services to the community with minimum disruption. He achieved his objectives in just a year.

The predictions of social catastrophe did not materialize. His level of high-quality engagement within his department was in many ways matched by his fellow senior civil servants. The approach was engagement and transparency. His approach was replicated. Through so doing, the effectiveness and contribution of other civil service leaders who also faced stringent budget cuts was enhanced. The greater the success and respect of the civil servant within his team, the more he was admired by his senior colleagues who were learning about the practical value of EQ. His transparency and sharing were emulated through many parts of the Civil Service.

Eventually the civil servant left and is now pursuing a successful career in the private sector. Even those former colleagues who disliked him were sorry to see him go. His EQ legacy lives on.

Sometimes there is no escaping resentment. Irrespective of the person's level of EQ accomplishment, any challenge will cause resentment in some people. What is important is the ability to spot resentment and understand what has created such negative emotions. This provides a better chance of breaking through barriers between people and emerging with more positive relationships.

When people take different positions, this can create resentment, resulting in them being marginalized, pushed to one side or even fired. This can happen regardless of whether they are in the top team, the board, general management or even if they are excellent at what they do. So much depends on mindset. Those who genuinely want to do a good job, those focused on value delivery, tend to have little time for negativity, especially if it is persistent. They may get angry, but that irritation dissipates quickly. Those who take insult on being challenged and feel marginalized and undermined when their proposition is scrutinized are more likely to harbour deep resentment. As stated, such powerful emotions can last a lifetime.

Interestingly, some resentment may remain in the realm of 'I don't like you, but it's not so important because I can at least respect what you are doing.' For some it is difficult in a team to respect someone they don't like even when the team is working on an EQ-type basis. So dislike, resentment and lack of respect can all roll into one.

Imagine soccer players who refuse to pass the ball to their star player because they don't like him and don't want him to succeed. This problem can't be solved on the playing field. Instead it is dealt with in the players' room and in training. It may even result in the team getting rid of the star player who, despite being great, simply cannot work well with others.

Similarly, if there is someone in the boardroom who is consistently damaging in their comments, irrespective of how right they might be, then regardless of their skills, others may simply not pass the ball to them. Resentment, negative emotions and performance mean that even the best player in the team can suddenly find themselves on the outside.

She did me a favour

A long-standing feud between two senior managers in a world-renowned NGO led to one complaining about the other to the CEO. 'He is never here! He's always outside chasing something or other! He's not contributing!' she criticized. The CEO asked to see the 'absent' protagonist. It became apparent that the individual had been productive in making contacts and securing long-term deals that made the NGO more secure. However, the protagonist was also unpopular. The CEO questioned him about whether he thought the NGO was capable of survival. The protagonist responded that the NGO was in a financially precarious situation and someone had to win contracts, and that meant being constantly outside.

Despite his best efforts, the CEO felt that the example given by the protagonist was not in keeping with what was required of a senior manager and demanded that he spend more time addressing internal issues. The protagonist disagreed and promptly submitted his resignation. He departed as soon as was convenient. Currently, the NGO faces considerable financial loss and is likely to be wound down.

Reflecting on the matter afterwards, the protagonist said of his former colleague, 'She did me a favour! She got me out of the organization when I didn't have the strength to leave.'

Some individuals are able to put aside their resentment, but only if they have the maturity to do so. How much do they care, and can they step away from something which hasn't gone well? Once it is clear that the intentions were good and that a positive mindset has been achieved, a functioning EQ platform has been reached. At this point it is possible to enter into more meaningful discussion. But, be warned, the causes of resentment are rarely forgotten. The solution is more to do with how such emotions are positioned and dealt with. Without a positive and forward looking mindset and intent, negative sentiments are difficult to displace in favour of addressing future concerns.

Feedback

Critical to EQ is feedback, or the offering of information about each other to each other. Feedback is inevitably given during the building and management of relationships. Smart leaders provide a commentary that is much more measured, deeper in its analysis and essential to improving performance. When levels of trust and respect for others are high, and resentment is minimized, it is much easier to assess what upsets those whom you are trying to enhance, or identifying when someone is not ready for a task or not even ready to listen to your feedback.

It takes a number of steps to arrive at the point where information can be given to others so that relationships improve. This happens after emotions on both sides have been handled so that both parties are now ready to listen to genuine comment. Many EQ theorists suggest that giving deep, meaningful feedback as part of a performance review much earlier in the process is a key part of creating an EQ environment. However, our research suggests that determining people's preparedness to receive and positively handle feedback is a much more important consideration. It is commonplace to see people with a low EQ capacity giving feedback haphazardly. If they have a high IQ but low EQ, it is likely their feedback will be both deeply accurate and yet possibly resented.

The chairman of a well-known European company received a distraught letter of complaint from a senior female administrator stating that the CEO had been having an affair with her, but had broken the relationship off in favour of his wife. She threatened to go to the press unless something was done. The chairman immediately called on the CEO in order to find out the truth. Yes, an affair had taken place and, yes, the CEO wished to end the relationship, deeply regretting the harm he had done to both his wife and his temporary mistress.

In his chat with the chairman it also transpired that the CEO had an unhappy private life. Concerned about the likely reputational damage, the chairman seriously considered asking the CEO to leave the company. However, the CEO happened to be very good at his job and had steered the company through a number of distinctly difficult market conditions. The chairman decided that it was time for the CEO to be more professional and not allow his private life to detract from his professional contribution. He needed to give the CEO feedback on what he was like as a person and what he needed to do to win the chairman's confidence. This was no easy matter as the CEO was sensitive to criticism and in many ways vulnerable to further emotional setbacks due to the unsatisfactory nature of his personal relationships.

The chairman decided to take the following steps in offering feedback to arrive at a resolution on whether the CEO was going to stay or leave:

Step 1 – Nurturing comfort

It was important for the chairman to make the CEO feel sufficiently comfortable so that the feedback that needed to be given could be done with the resulting buy-in. So the chairman talked around the subject of the CEO and his performance and the contribution he had made to the company until a level of intimacy was realized and the two could talk more openly to each other.

Step 2 – Talk around the challenges

Rather than approaching the sensitive question of the CEO's private life, the chairman talked around the challenges of balancing private and work life. The chairman said that he too faced tensions in trying to balance home and work life, and that these tensions never went away, but were simply managed situation by situation. The resilience to cope and the patience to help the family deal with the stresses and strains of executive life require patience, tact and, most of all, visible care and concern.

Step 3 – Self-admission

Now the CEO felt both comfortable and able to admit the challenges he faced and his own shortcomings. Yes, he was at fault and accepted responsibility for that, and, yes, he was prepared to resign if the chairman so requested. The chairman thanked him for his honesty and said he valued his contribution as CEO and that to replace him would be difficult. He would like him to stay, but on the condition that he resolve the complaint made by the female administrator.

Step 4 – Facing up to the consequences

The purpose in ensuring full engagement as part of the feedback offered is to help the other party face up to the consequences of their actions and to find ways to address the concerns they have. The CEO had to make up his mind between his wife or his mistress. He faced the distinctly uncomfortable circumstance of having to apologize to his female colleague and ask how their situation could be resolved, as the affair could not continue. As it turned out, the woman eventually resigned, but the CEO dealt with his circumstances entirely by himself. The affair became known in the organization, and he lost face.

In contrast, considerable admiration was shown to the woman for her courage in speaking up. Without saying so, the CEO made it evident that he was at fault and weathered the storm. He is still in post today, and still shoulders a tarnished reputation. When asked what he had learnt from the encounter, his response was twofold: admiration for the chairman, who showed the patience and sensitivity to help him be less defensive, and, second, to develop a level of resilience that the CEO felt he never had by facing up to the circumstances.

An EQ culture

EQ helps people manage their own emotions and those of others through understanding context and people, handling resentment and utilizing feedback effectively. Eventually, it creates a wider, more supportive culture.

In our experience, mission-based organizations are more likely to encourage a deep level of engagement and ongoing dialogue with stakeholders. This is logical because these organizations are focused on delivering value to their stakeholders – and to do so requires them to understand what their stakeholders (customers, employees, suppliers) are actually experiencing. In a vision-based organization, in contrast, the priority is to get stakeholders to agree with the leaderships' value proposition and support the vision.

Both Caterpillar and Deutsche Telekom have created EQ-type environments in challenging market conditions. The reality is that growing an EQ culture is fraught with difficulties due to the differences between people, a lack of aligned thinking, personal agendas and distaste of each other at top management levels. Yet certain organizations have addressed such tensions. To do so demands sensitive and forward-looking leadership.

Such has been the case with Caterpillar, a major multinational business operating in the highly competitive construction, energy and mining equipment sector. The company has avoided mass redundancies by adapting from one change of technology to another, while holding its organization together. The secret to its success? The Caterpillar culture and the values held dear by staff and management. Caterpillar has worked hard to understand its staff and clients, and hasn't rushed the process. The business took a step-by-step approach to building its deep-rooted culture and resisted demands from external stakeholders to change to realize short-term results. This is an example of EQ at its best.

When asked, one of the senior managers in Caterpillar told us that creating a culture of positive engagement requires time and nurturing in order to provide defence of the deep-seated values of respect and concern for people. In fact, the values of Caterpillar, all embracing as they are, essentially hinge on one core theme: quality. Quality of product, quality of service, quality of organization and quality of internal and external relationships. For Caterpillar, spotting where things go wrong and dealing with them in an EQ fashion is as important as getting the strategy right.

One Caterpillar executive identified the key components of its much-admired culture as

- living the values of the company, particularly quality, since its inception in 1917;

- having meaningful engagement with internal and external stakeholders;

- showing deep respect in dealings with all;

- fostering transparency and equity;

- dealing with operational issues, strategy, values and responsibilities to people as something all rolled into one way of working; and

- valuing stewardship as the fundamental approach to leadership.

These two organizations, and others like them, operate with a certain set of intrinsic employee human rights built into their structures and culture. There is a right to be listened to, to offer comment which contributes to quality and to be respected by others. All of these factors ultimately result in providing outstanding service, but only a few organizations have made the link between what they do, human rights, and improved outcomes. Such conditions tend to flourish under a form of inspired leadership called 'stewardship', an all-embracing care and concern for people and the wider organization.

Similarly, the German telecommunications company Deutsche Telekom has avoided the fate of British Telecom (BT), which has suffered widespread redundancies and been plagued by complaints about poor service, despite both organizations essentially being in the same business. Deutsche Telekom's service mentality has been a key factor in distinguishing it from what many see as BT's lack of attention towards its clients. In a service-oriented business, within the context of a fast-moving technology market, creating an EQ culture should be the norm for any organization that wants to achieve a pathway to sustainable success.

Bullying and harassment

Living and harnessing the core values of the organization is one side to developing an effective EQ culture. The other is confronting the increasing incidence of bullying and harassment. While the full picture is unclear, our experience suggests that bullying is increasing dramatically across organizations of all sizes and sectors.

Bullying is abusive social interaction between peers, and between peers and their bosses, which can feature aggression, harassment and even violence. It is usually repetitive in nature and carried out by those who are in a position of power over the victim.

A growing body of research illustrates a significant relationship between bullying and EQ. Low EQ, sometimes in the bully or their victim, appears to be directly linked to involvement in bullying, or part of a relentless pursuit of short-term targets which dehumanize the work environment.

EQ education can substantially minimize bullying and support intervention initiatives. The exception is when harassment is institutionalized through, for example, the relentless pursuit of transactional targets. Where a culture of meeting targets at all costs predominates, a redesign of the enterprise is required, which is a topic dealt with in later chapters.

Short-term and overzealous attention to costs usually ensures that EQ cultures are not desired or respected. The first reason for this is that EQ culture does not produce quick or short-term results. Second, in a short-term market, assertiveness and being pushy are desired attributes, which naturally undermine relationship building. Third, when an organization has over-elaborate command and control structures, such as the UK's National Health Service (NHS), nurturing people and a teamwork culture is subordinate to adhering to procedures and protocol. To get an NHS appointment in the UK you have to go to your general practitioner (GP), who then writes a letter to an intermediary, who in turn responds to another doctor, who subsequently writes back to the original GP, who finally gets you onto a two-month waiting list. And all of this only happens if you are lucky.

In Germany, by comparison, this same action requires a brief phone call, and two hours later the relevant doctors will see you. The structural constraints witnessed in the UK system are bypassed in

Germany through resources being focused on delivering patient care. In contrast, in the UK a mass of management is devoted specifically to monitoring costs, which substantially increases overhead and by its very nature diverts attention from front-line services. In a culture such as this, EQ is effectively killed off, and the employees attracted to this type of environment tend to value controls. By implication, bullying can all too easily become a quick and easy way of getting things done.

Continued exposure to a culture of harassment leads to people believing that such an experience is normal. As a result, when they are accused of bullying and harassment, people often simply cannot believe it. Yet if you watch their behaviour, the issue is quickly clear. They often think they are doing the best for the company, and say that if there weren't someone like themselves dealing with, and driving through, unpleasant decisions, then the organization would falter and decline. Others who do not bully say the same kind of thing, but their behaviour is based on a well-reasoned case with transparent and respectful instruction to others, despite the pressure of circumstances. It is these latter individuals who are the genuinely exceptional performers.

The norm in harassment cultures is bullying occurs throughout the organization. This does not mean that bullying in these cultures is not dealt with. It is. Incidents of bullying lower down the management hierarchy can be handled by adherence to company protocols or on a case-by-case basis. That is, if they come to the surface. The concern with harassment cultures is the low incidence of reported bullying, owing to a high level of fear about losing one's job or being stigmatized.

Bullying and harassment where initiated by the CEO or top manager for the purpose of bringing out the perceived best in an enterprise is a highly sensitive issue to address. What is viewed as being 'best to meet targets' often results in a culture which desperately needs greater transparency and teamwork in order to continue functioning. A sense of initiative and innovation are eroded. People's confidence diminishes. The organization very slowly declines, but like the 'frog in ever hotter water', those inside become used to this form of operation. Those who are more resilient and capable leave. What is most distressing is how many stay and feel that being emotionally abused is a normal experience.

Fundamentally EQ

Regardless of whether EQ is more naturally ingrained in some individuals, while having to be learnt by others, it is undoubtedly a fundamental work and life skill. What you understand about yourself through others can only be bolstered by developing related qualities even further.

When EQ becomes a part of the organizational mission, it raises performance to a different level. The dominance of the John Lewis Partnership is due to it being the best at providing service. As a result, Waitrose, a part of John Lewis, has become the fastest-growing food retailer in the Unite Kingdom. Similarly, Caterpillar is the leader in its field due to its deeply held value of quality. Of the few organizations genuinely utilizing EQ, they do so as an inherent good, and in so doing deliver service and quality.

EQ has to be based on deeply held core values, and such organizations emerge rarely. In this sense EQ acts as a fundamental guide to the core values that leaders wish to instil within their organization. Yet few organizations have migrated to a position where it has become such a core value that everybody is able to be satisfied.

A more pragmatic CEO could naturally ask what value EQ has to offer. The reply can be difficult to justify, because the CEO's mindset often runs along the lines of 'I have to drive results through', and yet takes into account 'This isn't a business about being nice to people, it's a business about results.' Technically, this is true. Determining and justifying value can be difficult. The longer-term outcomes have to be emphasized, clearly showing the link between individual and team interactions, and the desired result, which is unlikely to be a short-term gain. The positive effect of EQ is in growing a culture that is sensitive to pursing opportunities. No immediate outcome can be guaranteed, but both staff and management are ready to put their differences to one side, discuss matters openly and choose whatever opportunities arise as they are created.

There is a fine line dividing bullying from assertiveness as a means of keeping the workforce appropriately focused. If a CEO is achieving the required results, but people are constantly leaving and being replaced, it becomes difficult to accurately judge the success of an organization.

EQ's value is defined by the levels of service, motivation and successful interaction with clients and stakeholders that can be achieved. It has greater meaning where a hard strategy exists around products or costs, because the EQ argument benefits a culture where people work more effectively together and provide better service.

The undeniable point about EQ is that you cannot say that treating people well is going to make your organization perform poorly in any sense.

Consider Ryanair, which has a hard-edged reputation for managing customer expectations and service. By comparison, Caroline McCall, CEO of its arch-competitor, EasyJet, came to the business with no experience of airlines and created a company that is probably slightly more expensive in terms of comparable flights than Ryanair, but is seen as considerably more successful on customer service. How has this been achieved? McCall was appointed in part because of her extensive experience in customer service, having previously been CEO of the Guardian Media Group, which has a trust that protects the *Guardian* newspaper's ability to express independent opinion, unlike many other papers.

On taking the EasyJet role, one of McCall's first actions was to fly the company's routes around the world, after which she concluded that if staff and the whole system were just a little bit more service oriented, and customers weren't left scrambling for their seats, then additional costs would be minimal but retention would reach maximum levels.

The European no-frills airline EasyJet is an excellent illustration of how even the most impossible situations can be turned around by the values of the CEO or chairperson through the creation of an EQ environment. McCall's mindset is one of value delivery. She measured things and gathered evidence before going to the board and saying, 'This is the proposition', flying everywhere while critics questioned why she wasn't in the office. In a saturated, cost-driven market, McCall went completely against the grain. This is EQ in action.

EQ requires that we're all singing from the same hymn sheet. The analogy is that can do EQ well in a football team, but that you can't use it well in the boardroom of a football club because the team all pull together to score goals (a singular objective), but the board is there for the football, for making money and for running the business (multiple objectives), so EQ doesn't work well.

As the football analogy suggests, the problem with EQ is that it doesn't seem to work that well at senior management levels because misalignment takes place when leaders can't agree on the most important objective (winning football matches or balancing the books) or competitive advantage differentiation. In contrast, Caterpillar and EasyJet highlight EQ as a critical boardroom issue through effectively taking the longer-term perspective, having a clear sense of mission and nurturing a performance-oriented safety-factor culture for the greater majority.

Action points

The skills of EQ – how we form relationships and trust one another, how we're open with each other, how we use charm – are essential to building a strong team.

Assessing your leadership EQ:

- How can you engage meaningfully and deeply so that trust is built in your organization and authenticity is allowed to flourish?

- What is the single unifying objective that your leadership aims to achieve?

- If there are multiple objectives associated with your role, how can you deploy EQ to support those objectives without undermining your authenticity?

- Who are the key people you need to deliver value and how can you use your EQ to support them?

3

PQ: Working through politics

Trained both as a lawyer and as an engineer, Jilly had a quiet disposition and a disarmingly sharp mind. In many ways, she was the last person anyone would consider a political player. She was also the first woman to be appointed chairman of a prestigious information technology (IT) company. The former chairman also held the role of CEO. He had left the enterprise wealthy but also with a questionable reputation related to quality of service and delivery. His growth strategy was impressive. Bonuses were awarded to the favoured high performers. In the middle of all this, service, teamwork and duty of care were lost. Both the government and shareholders recognized this and on his departure separated the role of chairman from CEO. As the new chairman, Jilly recognized the overwhelming need to re-establish the values of service and care for the community.

'In this our new phase, I ask you all to contribute to this board and especially to express your views openly. I do not want a board divided. For this reason I do want contribution and a sense of cabinet responsibility to the decisions we reach.'

Jilly knew that old habits die hard but slowly worked to induce a board culture of open discussion. Yet the one-to-one behind-the-scenes meetings between individual directors continued, albeit less frequently than with the previous chairman. She recognized that contradictory ways of doing things were deeply ingrained in the company, and that the non-executives were quite happy to live with two different ways of operating. So she decided to do the same.

At a future board review and as part of our research, the non-executives confided about what progress was being made.

'Yes, she is good, really good. There is a new buzz in the boardroom. We are really now addressing what we had previously ignored. We challenge the management, but positively, and they confide they have benefited from this. She knows what she wants and she knows how to get it, but even she has changed. Sometimes she is powerful at board meetings; sometimes she has a quiet chat or dinner with some of us privately. She is open and closed, a team player and a politician. It is done so well. We love it!'

Jilly, who insisted on being called the 'chairman' as a statement that she was no different to anyone else, commented,

'Well, that's a sign of a good board. They really do know what is happening. One of the interesting things I have learnt about being chairman is that I really do see everything. I see where strengths lie and where weaknesses prevail. So it is up to me to shape a common understanding on this board, and this learning has not been easy. To improve things in the company, I must have total engagement from the board. So with the sensitive issues, I look at my board and wonder when we will get closure on this topic. Sometimes that could be nine months ahead. So I think about twelve board meetings into the future. In between I do what it takes to reach that full agreement, even though others may think I behave strangely. But I never compromise on my ethics and values. My intentions are always honourable, and I believe that it is why my colleagues accept me and allow me to do the things I do.'

Politics is about negotiating the impossible to the possible. It also means drawing on the EQ skill sets of sensitivity and empathy, which should be adopted in circumstances where there is a misalignment of interests. In this sense, politics is about reshaping thinking, especially when open conversation is not likely to work. So politics is EQ, but with an agenda.

The quest for the possible

Politics is essentially the negotiation of the impossible to the possible. It is a process of discussion, either overt or covert, which takes place in order to reach some sort of agreement, harmony or way forward, particularly when agendas have become misaligned. It involves dealing with complexities and diversities when few are willing to shift position. It is the ultimate process of negotiation that brings together the light and dark challenges of organizational life.

If your role is that of CEO or head of department, it is your job to pull various teams together in order to achieve an alignment of thinking and systems. This allows resources to be used effectively to meet targets, goals and objectives.

This finely tuned balancing act is called politics. It also involves negotiation between a number of different 'logics', many of which can on their own make eminent sense, but when brought together there is an incompatibility. The fact that these logics are incompatible doesn't matter. You have to deal with the interrelationships between people who often have very different interests. Politics is a negotiation.

A further political arena exists between the internal organization and the external demands placed upon it. The internal organization includes everyday processes, systems and the essential structure of business. External demands will often cut across all of this, which begs the question, 'How is it possible to satisfy my client when we have purchasing procedures and protocols where people's expenses can't even be paid on time?'

This necessitates a process which understands and appreciates that politics is essentially a negotiation involving a particular way of thinking and a series of key steps and behaviours. The political manager is someone who is deeply concerned with delivering value because they understand the sensitivity involved in working across a number of different cultures and mindsets which are not aligned. They are also aware that this situation is not going to change, and have to balance this against the view of others who see politics as nasty, dirty and not delivering value.

The reality is that we are all politicians. Everyone in an organization exists in a political world. They're all politicians – though some are more proficient than others.

This point is explained by Andrew Kakabadse in his previous book, *The Politics of Management*. American sociologists and political scientists recognized that the growing national and multinational organizations were, in fact, a mini replica of the sovereign state. Complexity, size and an array of interests need harnessing in order to have a company be competitive. Thus, the early work on politics and organizations came from the politics of community development, and one can see why: engagement across a multitude of interests is vital for the growth and prosperity of both the firm and the community.

And politics is personal. Think of the relationship between subordinate and boss, and the quality of the interrelationship between the two. A leader who is not politically astute can be highly damaging to one's career aspirations. How can a political accommodation be achieved when they don't agree? There can be style, ego and differences of perception at play. Add to this a personality which is overly rational and not engaging, as opposed to someone who is so concerned with engagement they tiptoe everywhere, and you are left with approaches that can result in a loss of respect because the boss doesn't offer clear direction, or empathy for your circumstances.

John, a well-intended and respected man, was overly reliant on numbers. The numbers were clearly captured and the case put forward logical. But John left his audience cold. This led to a crisis. His dealing with a customer complaint started with him reiterating numbers, but his proposal was brought to an abrupt halt by a customer irate that his feelings were ignored and his situation not understood. The customer left the meeting making it clear that he would lodge a complaint with John's boss.

That day was not John's boss's day. Another member of John's team had been fighting hard to have one of their talented up-and-coming performers be promoted. At the talent meeting, a number of managers were each championing their protégé hard. In order to smooth over the distemper in the room, that one up-and-coming talented individual was put on the waiting list for next year's promotions in favour of someone else's protégé. It just so happened that the irate customer stormed to John's boss's office and was followed by the manager whose protégé was disappointed. Some days being politically adept does not always work.

Why rationalism detests politics

The word 'politics' comes from the ancient Greek *polis*, or 'the people'. It is nothing more than the interrelationships between people operating in different contexts. Taking these two concepts into account, it is possible to see how politics can offend rationalism in a big way. It begs the question that those at the top are not always right. Rationalism detests politics, because whatever is being done is fundamentally open to questioning.

Why do so many people struggle with the fact that politics is simply a reflection of complexity? In hindsight it is because many recognize that they have been both naive and driven in their decision-making by rationalism as a way of thinking.

As previously stated, in the business world rationalism was popularized in the 1920s by the Chicago School of Economics, drawing on the principles of scientific observation as epitomized by the work of Newton. A British tradition dating back to the eighteenth century, rationalism is about looking at something and measuring it. By doing so we arrive at a clearer understanding and establish a logical way forward by recognizing the truth.

In philosophical terms this is called positivism, or 'doing what's right', and this way of thinking has been imbued into business school students' behaviour across America, the UK, Europe and Asia for many years. However, there is a growing recognition that rationalism and positivism simply don't reflect the reality and reason of competitive advantage in the private sector, and value delivery in the public sector and NGOs.

The senior partner of a world-renowned consulting firm wanted to provide an 'all-round package solution' for their clients. The package involved delivering on service and then supported it by training. A nice idea, but it was never tested. Certain country partners supported this initiative. Others said it would not work here. The reason? The brand image of the firm in that locality. Training and development were not viewed in clients' eyes as a central offering of the firm. Be selective and see where such an initiative will work was the comment from the country partners.

That advice was ignored. The drive to recruit hundreds of high-priced training professionals began. Unable to deliver on this package, certain of the high-performing, high-fee-earning partners resigned and joined competitive firms. Certain ones stayed but resisted, and one by one were removed. A year later the firm lost 15 per cent of its highest fee-earning partners and over 600M US$ of business to competitors. The new package solution had to be scrapped. Total loss: 850M US$, and all for what? Because the senior partner did not recognize that in a complex services firm, competitive advantage means something different locality by locality. This is a classic rationalism versus contextualism clash.

There is not one logical platform that can be employed to guide complex, large and often international organizations. Instead, the alternative to positivism is contextualism, which was championed by the philosopher Aristotle. He said that you can rationalize as much as you want, but until you go into somebody's home, see how they live and reinforce their particular values, you have no understanding at all. It is contextualism, argued Aristotle, which drives people forward. Rationalism, in contrast, is a destructive concept that actually blinds you to the reality of what is in front of you.

What this means is that life and work consist of multiple contexts working together. Aristotle said that it takes a person of considerable skill and wit to navigate their way through this, requiring clarity of thinking and analysis to focus on a singular objective. Contextualism enables an individual to work their way through multiple interests so that they become aligned, and Aristotle popularized the political behaviours of individuals and city states as key mechanisms of creation and community. He observed that unless you are politically astute, you will get nowhere.

We are trained in rationalism at business schools, but we need to relearn all of our skills when we go to the top in terms of contextualism. What is the principle of rationalism as far as business and organizations are concerned when it applies to the public sector? Rationalism is fundamentally focused on getting the strategy right. You may not like the strategy, but that's what it is. Having got the strategy right, what then follows is structure and how the strategy should be executed. It is at this stage that engagement is attempted, and this is not about what you feel but rather what you will do and how the message is cascaded down the line.

Nobody questions that strategy is important, but what is equally important is whether organizations engage with reality because, until they do this, nothing is going to happen.

Working through politics

A new service line was being taken through the company's demanding quality control procedure. Would the new offering survive scrutiny? The managers in the firm knew that they could not penetrate this new market until due process was seen to be done. The comprehensive evidence-based case was scrutinized by a series of committees, each determining the viability of the new offering from the perspective of sales, marketing and product quality. Suggestions made for improvement were readily and positively adopted. Despite support from the rest of the organization, the director of quality control seemed unconvinced. Aside from requiring further scrutiny for the new offering, he took a long time to respond to emails and phone calls. He was even heard to say, 'This offering will not fly.' Despite strong evidence, the only way round the director of quality of control was lobbying and politicking. The team supporting the new service line had their friends in the organization agree to give their full support and that thought should convince the CEO. Equally, the director of quality control initiated his own separate campaign undermining the new offering. Mistrust grew. Colleagues found themselves browbeaten and so began to complain. Eventually, the CEO required that the new service offering go through a final stage of scrutiny. Approval was given, and that service offering is now offered to clients.

At first glance, the team championing the new service line won. In reality, however, nobody won. Relationships had become damaged and would take a long time to repair. In the meantime, support for new future products and services would not be forthcoming. Given the circumstances, the politics that were played made the negative outcome inevitable. Had the case been examined entirely on evidence, relationships would have stayed positive and professional. Instead, the politics became personalized. The lesson is 'steer away from personalized politics and be driven by evidence'. If nothing else, the nastiness that arises from negative politics is minimized.

In many organizations misalignment is routinely manifested in an abundance of organizational politics.

The true test is to ask the GMs two levels below what is really going on. Usually the story is quite different from what you hear at board level. You will often discover that politics is a reality, deeply embedded in the organization.

The *Oxford English Dictionary* defines politics as 'activities concerned with the acquisition and exercise of authority or government'. To some extent, politics is inevitable. But how can and should it be managed?

There are two principle mechanisms to consider. The first is power and the second is politics. Power is a lever, and it is vital to understand how to use it as part of a resource-building and dependency-creating exercise.

Politics demands contextual acceptance, because if you have not accepted what is happening after negotiations, there will likely be a worse problem than if negotiations had never begun in the first place. You will become more irritated because you will feel manipulated.

Power is different from politics to the extent that it involves the potential to use particular resources to achieve particular ends.

The conditions for power use

Power is likened to being a springboard from which to act. This means it is important to consider the conditions that influence the why, when and where to act. There are four key conditions:

1. Resources

Wielding power involves the use of resources. The resources can be under the control of an individual or organizationally based. Someone who has the authority to recommend the promotion or demotion of any one person, would classify such power as an organizational resource, and could exercise that power as an employee of the organization.

In contrast, personal resource power can range from wealth, intelligence and knowledge to physical appearance. Whichever resource power is utilized, the use of that power allows an individual to influence the thinking, behaviour and attitudes of others.

2. Dependency

The capability to influence others through the use of resources is achieved only if those being influenced need, or are attracted to, the resources in question. Requiring a particular resource is likely to make a person dependent on the resource wielder. For example, it is not uncommon for banks to influence senior management appointments in client organizations.

A consultant to a well-known investment bank in the City of London was invited to attend a dinner at which the senior managers of the bank were hosting the top management team of a company that was about to float its shares in the market. The bank was the agent in the flotation.

The evening passed smoothly, and the company managers and, for a period of time, the bank's director of corporate finance, the managing director (MD) of the bank and the CEO of the client company were deep in conversation. The consultant noticed that the CEO did not appear to be comfortable.

Apparently, the bank's director of corporate finance and the MD had clearly indicated to the CEO that if they were to approve and invest their money in the flotation, they would insist on him changing his finance director. They did not think the current finance director was up to the job. Despite the fact that the company was the client and that the CEO had personally appointed the finance director, the individual was fired. The CEO depended more on the resources of the bank than he did on his finance director.

3. Alternative sources of resources

The availability of alternative resources influences the ability of individuals to utilize power sources. If an individual can call on others who can provide alternative resources or channels of influence, the individual's dependence on their original source is reduced.

4. Contextual acceptance

The discussion in terms of the use of power resources is often confined to being between those who wield resources and those who need resources. However, there are many interested and influential onlookers. These stakeholders may or may not like the manner in which power is wielded, even though they may not be directly involved in any transaction. They may be offended if they witness behaviour which they consider inappropriate.

Therefore a further consideration is gaining the tacit permission of these 'general' stakeholders. If these significant individuals disapprove of what is happening, nothing is likely to arise immediately, but a body of opinion against the power wielder is likely to grow, marginalizing over time the individual and their influence. Basically, the message will be 'Don't do business with this guy!'

Consider the case of UK Labour party leader Jeremy Corbyn's approach to political leadership. In his first party conference as leader, he promised to embark on a new form of politics, aimed at creating a 'kinder' country.

Vowing to break the established hold of the political class, Corbyn said he wanted the views of regular people to be recognized, while calling for a 'more inclusive, bottom-up approach' in every community and workplace, not just at Westminster. He added that 'real debate, straight talking and honesty' were needed, not message discipline.

At his first Prime Minister's Questions, Corbyn made two key moves, calling for an end to 'Punch and Judy' politics and posing questions to Prime Minister David Cameron supplied by members of the public. In the first instance, the self-described democratic socialist called for an end to the theatrics between the Labour and Conservative leaders, instead opting for a less confrontational and more civilized debate.

The move won points from many voters disillusioned with the bickering and grandstanding in the House of Commons between the government and the opposition, rather than a more professional discourse on the issues at hand.

The questions Corbyn directed to Cameron that were tabled by Cobyn, were supplied by regular Britons – Marie on the lack of affordable housing; a housing association worker, Stephen, who warned about a reduction in staffing levels; and one from Paul on the cuts in tax credits.

The Labour leader explained, 'I have taken part in many events around the country and had conversations with many people about what they thought about this place, our Parliament, our democracy and our conduct within this place.

'Many told me they thought prime minister's question time was too theatrical, that Parliament was out of touch and too theatrical and they wanted things done differently, but above all they wanted their voice heard in Parliament.'

Oddly enough, and in contrast to what Corbyn said, power does not need to have contextual acceptance. A worker does not have to accept what a leader is doing, because the leader will do it in any case.

In this sense, political power is a personal thing that can be used negatively, and role and status may be utilized to seek inappropriate reverence from others. Without a process of engagement which recogniseizes and thanks others for their achievements, a power-driven leader will push things through, or use people to achieve their goals, or remove those they dislike. Power without politics results in a nasty and divisive culture. Alternatively, power can be a positive, developmental force that is concerned with people's progress and serves to create a cohesive culture. In such circumstances bureaucracy, contracts and subpoenas become of secondary value to trust and enthusiasm.

If the boss asks you to do something, but they don't believe in it and neither do you, you'll both sit and talk about it. Then you'll accept what you've been told, but ultimately the relationship will be damaged. You have to get on and do what you've been asked but you'll continue to ask, 'Why?'

In this sense politics is a must. We understand that power is essential to change structures and attitudes, and you may have to use your strengths and resources to rule people in or out of the process. But, if this isn't done well, how is it possible to ensure that an organization will become more sustainable and positive than it was previously?

Power without politics undermines the ability to win the necessary engagement to support a way forward. In effect, the bedding down process is ineffective and results in a disaffected organization. Alternatively, using a more subtle personal-engagement approach allows for a quite different result. There may be some pain involved in arriving at organizational outcomes, but people will look more positively towards the future. Bedding down and buy-in are overlapping parts of this journey. Buy-in is a personal process, where you personally buy in to what is happening. Bedding down is the cumulative process of buy-in from all those who are connected to the organization.

Part of bedding down is the working with and acceptance of the new structure, ways of operating, roles, tasks and reward systems. Buy-in is highly personal depending on what's happening to individual roles, whereas bedding down occurs as the organization gets used to wider changes and figures out how to make them work.

There is an interesting difference in how mission-based and vision-based organizations do politics. In a mission-based organization, politics is used as a means of managing misalignments and tensions over value delivery. It is the mechanism by which the reality of what's happening on the ground is transmitted to the leadership and vice versa – what the leadership requires of its stakeholders is also negotiated. In a vision-based organization, politics is the process by which different individuals seek to further their position and exert their will – vision – upon the rest of the organization.

The mission-based organization is more likely to experience the positive side to politics requiring working through complexities and stakeholders who are continually not aligned so that positive engagement emerges. The alternative is the destructive politics used to divide and isolate people to get your own way.

One of the key political areas is between governance and strategy. The question arises as to what governance is supposed to do in terms of its oversight, and what the top team or board is meant to do with respect to their strategy delivery thinking. Other important political areas also exist between the corporate centre and the operation of businesses, and the permanent secretaries and their respective civil service departments, as well as the director generals who each have different functions beneath them. These are the two fundamental points of political operation that need to be worked through.

The old theory followed that if an organization gets its strategy right, then everything else will work. This was something that was so deeply embedded into leaders' souls that it actually worked for a period of time. But even in the 1950s, things that should have happened didn't, and academics began to recognize that this was the case. They began to look for alternative answers in the work of political analysts and discovered that the political conditions and processes needed to engage with different interests in local, rather than national, communities almost exactly mirrored the circumstances of continually expanding corporations.

This same thinking was not applicable to family businesses – largely because they do not generally feature complexity, owing to their smaller size. However, it was recognized in the 1950s that political interactions between family members do take place in family businesses, and that, if not handled well, they can damage the business and also destroy the family.

From the 1950s on, politics in management began to be recognized as a topic in its own right. By the 1970s and 1980s a question mark began to be raised noting that covert behaviour was sometimes necessary to get people to come together and discuss what needed to be done. This offended rationalist thinking because by the 1990s global growth was slowly coming to an end. By the 1990s, which featured the beginnings of the financial crisis, commoditized markets had become saturated, innovation was drying up and money was being made through the control of costs.

By the late 1990s the centralization phenomenon had slowly but steadily taken hold, leading to a deeply controlling and often offensive philosophy. This in turn led to a politically negative perception of politics – so much so that it almost disappeared entirely from academic and management literature. Anyone who suggested that politics was something to be desired was labelled as negative, set on undermining the creation of wealth, the motivation of people, and the stability of teams. This was not the case. Politics is and was needed more than ever.

As the scandals arose with the dot-coms at the early turn of the century, followed by Enron and its ilk, people began to recognize that a pattern was emerging. All of these scandals showed a lack of logic at work, either on paper or in everyday practise. Something else was also happening beneath this vast global organizational infrastructure that was either being ignored or not taken into account: a deep mistrust of the organization, a lack of engagement and management not allowing itself to be challenged.

Value delivery through performance

'We have to build our reputation. It is not just us but the whole country. Foreign investors must have faith in our economy, and so we must address the concerns that all know, but no one dare raise.'

That was Ibrahim, chairman of one of the financial conduct authorities, in a particular Gulf State. Sensitive issue? Bribery and patronage! Of the two, patronage was the greatest threat for building trust with foreign investors.

Government was central to the appointment of the chairman of this authority. Government was also the source of patronage. However, Ibrahim was nobody's man. In the highly sensitive context of Middle Eastern politics, Ibrahim introduced performance assessment, not only for the staff and management but also for board members. Appointments were to be by merit, and he meant it.

A new wave of highly capable, professional staff and management nurtured a new performance-oriented culture, based on open conversation and feedback. Juniors challenged their seniors constructively.

Government at first seemed somewhat alarmed by the expressions of independence from the authority. However, noticing improvements in performance government took note. So did the chairmen of the banks in that country. For the first time, a wave of prosecutions of bank managers sent the message that the banks would comply with international rules. Pride in being professional, loyalty to the organization and its mission, high levels of engagement and a positive dialogue with all stakeholders became evident.

Of course, Ibrahim had to play the politics of keeping government sweet that of itself was a monumental task. But he did that, and the organization admired their chairman even more. This was a talented man winning against all odds.

Ibrahim's accomplishments were noticed, and he was appointed minister of state and is now introducing the same reforms in government that he achieved in that authority.

All of the organizations now look to their new chairman. Undoubtedly he is a talented individual, but doubt has crept in as to whether he can handle critical stakeholder relationships and still maintain independence.

One senior manager commented, 'Yes, clever man, but is he clever enough to outmanoeuvre those sharks out there [he was referring to certain chairpersons of banks]). Ibrahim was not political and straightforward. That is what he was like with us, but so politically brilliant with those out there that they thought he was non-political. My fear with the new chairman is that he will succumb and in doing so, he will not be able to tell us. The situation will be reversed. He will be political with us, but not with those out there! I just wish someone could get to him and tell him what his job is really all about.'

Despite all efforts, certain negotiations do not proceed well. An immovable confrontation looms. One or more parties may have to leave the organization. Making that break requires being ruthless. Yet, many C-suite executives warn that being ruthless and disrespectful leads to the loss of valuable friends. The high performer goes out of his or her way to be utterly respectful to those who take a contrary position, thanking them for their contribution but emphasizing the damage that might occur to both the top team and organization if fundamental differences of opinion continue. The more respectful the C-suite executive, the more likely others will leave of their own volition, often publicly supportive of the very person they opposed.

C-suite politics is no game. The future of the enterprise is at stake. Thus, politics is a deeply personal experience. Each does it his or her own way. Maintaining conversation under adverse circumstances is of prime importance. We have already seen how many C-suite executives, through no fault of their own, are accused of being inconsistent and inauthentic. Many acknowledge the inconstancy and put that down to the volatile nature of changing circumstances. Yet, few feel themselves inauthentic. To minimiseize such accusations, it is important to know oneself and recognize one's impact on others.

Understanding politics

Mary wanted to promote John. Philip was championing Celia. It is likely that only one would be promoted in the coming year. At the meeting, Mary extolled John's virtues, track record and skills. Philip did much the same with Celia, plus played the gender card – 'we need more women in senior management'. The appointments board looked to Mary to gauge her reaction. Her case was based on John's professionalism, and he certainly wanted his achievements to speak for themselves. Celia equally stated the same, but her boss added that extra dimension. What would you do? How would you handle that uncomfortable political situation of challenging a gender diversity issue? In Mary's shoes, how would you take the conversation forward?

Sometimes being proficient at politics does not work out. The culture simply does not want to shift. Frustration with the politics of the enterprise can lead to a deterioration in discipline and the relationship between members of the top management team, as witnessed in the case mentioned above. That really pushes missed messages down the line. The success formula of 'Engagement X Alignment' becomes unbalanced.

Not knowing what to do with the negative interactions that now become part of the culture, many CEOs and top directors give undue attention to structures, processes and procedures. That is their way of handling tensions and counterproductive behaviour. From all of the studies we have conducted, the overwhelming evidence is that in such organizations, no matter how much money is spent on alignment, engagement still remains zero and so the end result is still zero. The only way to address engagement concerns is to face up to them and work through them.

The newly appointed CEO of a world-renowned multinational was told that the GM of Asia, based in Hong Kong, was the most difficult of all the regional GMs. The GM, Anjit, ran a tight ship, and in fact, was the highest-performing GM in terms of sales, profitability, cost control and marketing push. However, Anjit did not adhere to many of the corporate centre procedures. Although supposedly the most ruthless of the GMs, his people's scores outshone all others. The CEO visited Hong Kong and found a well-run organization that resisted numerous corporate centre processes: 'Your centre guys do not know how to run a business. Their politics and their corporate governance process undermined my profitability.' The team members around Anjit warned the CEO that their boss would leave if he was restrained much further. Even Anjit commented, 'When I go, the corporate guys will come down on to Hong Kong, pushing their procedures, reducing profitability and then blame me for the loss of performance.' Sensing that the new CEO was in two minds about Anjit, and that the pressure for centre procedures to be adopted would be increased, Anjit left. As he predicted, the division was 38 per cent down on target, and the corporate centre executives did not fail to remind the CEO of Anjit's resistance and now ultimate fall in performance. Unable to give clear direction one way or the other, the CEO was viewed as weak.

Of course, not all interactions and negotiations are political. Many are straightforward, where 'normal' rules of engagement hold. The trouble is that for the C-suite executive, normality and predictability are rare. The challenge is to turn the abnormal into extraordinary success. Aligning polar opposite interests is not a form of Machiavellianism. It is a core C-suite skill. Working through incompatibilities and irrational behaviour requires high levels of moral worth, sensitivity of style and a deeply powerful intellect.

Whistle-blowers, for better or worse, were removed. Paul Moor, former head of risk at HBOS, was not an outsider to his organization.

He carried out a survey to illustrate that HBOS was deeply vulnerable and could go bankrupt and, as a result, was sacked for not being a team player. He had broken the ethos of how we work together as a team. Similarly, David Kelly, the scientist and expert on biological warfare, was treated terribly by those in a position of power who were intent on making the case for war with Iraq, to the point where he committed suicide. From government to the private sector there is a distaste for contextualism and in particular the truth. The truth that most worrying those in power is that on the ground, in effect the point at which strategy is delivered and executed.

With all of these developments, people are now no longer as naive. If they are, regretfully, they will be hurt. The general recognition is that there is a complexity at work here that is not easy to handle and that, just because an organization might have called in consultants (which means nothing), there is a big process to manage once all the clever thinking is done, and this is about making it all work.

Today, even this process is still not fully understood. Few consultancy agencies focus on strategy execution as a principle service. Their mantra is more along the lines of 'we generate the strategy, get the structures and HR systems right, and we might help you implement some of this'. People have become more cynical, however, and recognize the complexity that will be required to make strategy – they question what action will need to be taken to make a plan work. The cynicism involved is 'Number one, you never asked me. Number two, if you had, I could have told you this wasn't going to work. Number three, you never wanted to ask me, and actually you don't care if it works or not. It's your view and you will make it happen.'

This links with the three power levers that can be brought into play. The first is, 'This is what needs to happen.' The second is, 'This is what's going to happen, but I would like you to have the idea first by planting an idea that is actually mine.' The third lever is when 'your ability to ask an alternative question is reduced, whether because you do not know what it is, or it is too embarrassing to ask'. The political player always uses the third lever, steering their audience away from asking an alternative question.

If people were not so cynical and were more aware of what is happening, there would be massive disappointment on their part. They would question how massive organizational failures are allowed to happen and would be in a state of constant surprise and disbelief at some leader's actions. There would be even more of an anti-politics reaction, but times have changed and beliefs and expectations have become predisposed towards failure.

What was particularly interesting about Donald Trump's successful bid for the American presidency is that, regardless of whether you dislike how he speaks or what he stands for, he had an undeniable impact in terms of engagement. Trump recognized that there are two or three fundamental sentiments that he could capture with a large swathe of the American population. The first is the idea that the country was declining. The second is that America should be great, and the third is that you as an individual could have a role to play in solving these challenges. He explained this brilliantly by capturing people's imagination through the use of simple words that translated into what this situation meant for them. If you want an exercise in how to realize engagement, watch him speak to an audience. Regardless of the controversial nature of his presidency, his initial impact has been remarkable. However, lacking in substance and being inconsistent, his staying power is now under severe threat.

In reality, it is not so much poor decision-making that causes organizational decline but more managerial inaction. Feeling inhibited from speaking out, and therefore doing little, is the root cause of organizational inadequacy.

At the same time it is important to recognize that taking action without fully understanding the nature and value of politics, means that it becomes impossible to implement the seven necessary steps required to achieve political success. These are detailed as follows.

The seven steps to political success

Step 1

Step 1 in politics is to get onto the same wavelength of the people you are dealing with. What is it that they want to hear, and how do they want to hear it? Then give them this message and take them with you, even if they do not know where the journey will end. Communication and intent are divorced, so you don't have to declare intent to get onto people's wavelength.

Step 2

Step 2 is to map out the agendas that you have to face, deal with, contend with, remove or integrate.

Continuing with Trump as an example, observe how he talks about the agendas of his competitors in such a way that many people can relate to it – first, because what he says about them is often true; second, because it is powerful; and third, because it is so clear. His rhetoric flows easily, and the clarity of his agendas, particularly in the Republican presidential primaries, were head and shoulders above those of his competitors. This was really no fool at work. In an organization you have to map out the agendas held by the top team and the board, and then respect them. These are the hurdles that have to be overcome if something is going to happen. Yet time catches up with you. Initial, impactful engagement needs to be followed up through case-based evidence. Trump's early success is now burdened by how he will follow up on his promises. His rhetoric is not matched by evidence-based policy.

Step 3

Step 3 is to bring everybody close to you. Get them involved in debates, and bring them into seminars and meetings. See what their reaction is and how different circumstances play out.

Imperfect leaders tend to get the strategy right, then follow with structure and cascade the message down the line. However, anyone who doesn't agree with them is out. They split the board and top team, and allow the political process to be seen as a nasty, divisive beast in action. This divide-and-conquer approach might begin with agendas being mapped out and political scenarios correctly assessed, but when the ultimate result is political gamesmanship, then all can see that in reality little or no political thought has been given to the consequences. It is just a crude and deliberate use of power.

When you are emotionally close to somebody, you discuss things. To begin with, you might dislike the person, but if they listen to you, then a growing respect begins to emerge. The whole point of bringing people closer together is to get them to listen to each other. This process is also focused on positioning agendas, which is the most subtle use of power.

Step 4

Step 4 involves a shifting of mindsets, which is essentially how to nudge, rather than push, people into a new way of thinking. This is achieved through being personal, by sitting together in informal meetings, by sharing stories and getting people involved so that they want to take responsibility. There is a manipulative element to this, but it is done with the best of intentions.

Step 5

Step 5 overlaps to some extent with Step 4. If you remember the Spycatcher trial, you may also recall that a civil servant who went to Australia to give evidence in connection with the case was later described in newspapers as being 'economical with the truth'. This phrase represents one of the world's most subtle concepts. It was originally constituted into British history and popularized by the parliamentarian Edmund Burke in the eighteenth century. He effectively said that when dealing with any area of complexity, you should be very careful about the information released and how it is positioned.

At the time, Britain was one of the most powerful nations in the world, with an Empire that stretched from Canada to India. It controlled half of Africa and was the envy of Europe. Why would such a political and geographical force have any concerns about being 'economical with the truth?' Quite simply, because they thrived on continually asking the question 'How do we handle this in such a way that it all still works?' Burke's comment cut to the heart of about how we deal with complexity.

Information is often positioned in order to get people to think in one particular way. Former UK prime minister Margaret Thatcher popularized this approach when she stated that there was no alternative for Britain to the market-based economy, adding that it was not a market-based economy such as the Germans operated in, but instead should be based on the American model.

At this point in the public's thinking, there was no alternative to a US-style, market-based economy. There was no outcry or adverse reaction to suggest that there were two market-based economies to choose from, despite London and Frankfurt being only an hour's flight apart, and with the latter having a far superior financial set-up when compared with the UK. This was the result of nobody thinking this way because positioning information is a vital political skill.

Step 6

None of this works unless you are doing Step 6 all of the time. This is where you recognize and realize the legitimacy of the networks in which you are operating. You do not push people. Instead you have meetings, visit various departments and have coffee breaks and conversations. During all of this you are trying to integrate the legitimacy of your position and agendas with you as an individual. You can divorce politics from the concept, but if you are not personally legitimized, others will automatically reject the idea.

Rationalization talks about ideas or the concept. Politics reviews the legitimization among individuals, and how we gain legitimacy in our various networks. If a poor leader is in favour with all of the critical departments they want to be, and then nudges away the departments they don't need, all that's needed is one scandal to bring the entire operation down. Legitimization through networks is internal and external. What is interesting about power players is that they see legitimization as being external because they have repositioned their assets internally. However, they have not accounted for how badly a demotivated or demoralized organization can bring an operation down.

What's particularly interesting about the political player's legitimization through networks is that the process is physically and mentally exhausting. It is incredibly tiring in practise, so you have to delegate. It is impossible to deal with everything; therefore, you must have a very good team around you who believe in what is happening. For the power operator, this is not necessary. The team does what they are told because of an assumption that tasks and structures are clear. The power leader is often charismatic. This is because they only deal with one or two things and then make a big announcement while hogging the limelight. The political player may or may not be charismatic, but they are identifiable in the essence of how they operate across their networks. They listen, and how can you listen without having humility?

A newly appointed CEO of a charity, after a short time in post, emphasized that sales was the strategy to pursue. She stated, 'We need to sell our services, and a more subtle marketing and brand approach cannot work.' The former chairman did not agree and had tried to expose the board members to various influential stakeholders in order to attract donations. The former chairman had convinced the board of the brand's strength, even the superiority of the organization. Unable to reach agreement with her chair, the new CEO was ready to walk, a prospect no one on the board wanted as they recognized the devotion and energy of the CEO to the charity. After some discussion, the chairman resigned, and the first action of a newly appointed chairman was to extensively listen to the CEO. More sales effort, more door to door, more fetes and garden parties. Nice expensive brochures sent through the post will add little value, stated the CEO. Despite the support of the CEO by the new chairman, the board members were sceptical. In order to reach alignment, the chairman listened to all the arguments but only emphasized two points: be guided by the evidence, and have the values of the charity guide all strategic decisions and actions. 'We must fund our projects ethically', said the chairman. The chairman's approach slowly won the board round. Now the CEO feels that she has the full support of the board. When asked how he shaped the mindset of the board, the chairman responded, 'Handling the politics was tricky, as I had to be seen, to not be playing politics in the first place. The evidence spoke for itself, but I had to have the board recognize that we are not as grand as we imagined. It was the recognition that our values are sound that allowed me to work my way through these tricky relationships.'

Step 7

Step 7 is about knowing yourself in terms of the mixed messages that you may give out. It is important to understand the reality of how other people are going to perceive you, which involves knowing how you communicate messages, and what others hear and understand. This type of deep insight was exemplified by the writings of Aristotle, who said that you cannot be a leader until you have deep insight into yourself. This is a real dichotomy for strategy literature as at times you do have to be ruthless, certain people do not fit in and it is critical that they are moved out, so you have to be respectful as well as hard-edged.

The political player doesn't have to be liked, but they do need to be respected. Once that respect is there actions, such as the necessary removal of people, can be balanced against the logic and clarity of why and how such activities are happening. This actually creates further growth of respect, because then all can see that a considered view has been taken on things, that you have done all that you can and that it is not working so we have got to move on.

The power player is quick, charismatic and easy to read. The political player is slow, humble and complex. The latter's actions may be considered necessarily 'deceptive', which is a potentially negative side to politics. Take time to understand your organization and how its politics work. Ask yourself, 'What the purpose of politics?' If it is to bring systems and people together to realize value delivery and enhance competitive advantage, then you are on the right path.

Assessing your leadership PQ

In many ways PQ is the follow on from EQ. When EQ doesn't work anymore, leaders are forced into negotiating.

- The skills of EQ – how we form relationships and trust with one another, how we're open with each other, how we use charm – we also use in PQ. The difference is that with PQ, the leader has an agenda. What is your agenda?

- With EQ, the agenda is us working together as a team. So with PQ, it is a case of being EQ visible and not making it too obvious that you are being political in these circumstances. How will you play the politics – openly or covertly?

- The other part of PQ is that you have no choice. There are certain circumstances you walk into when the only way out is to negotiate: you have to negotiate as best you can, and you have to be as authentic as possible. What negotiating style will you deploy?

4

RQ: The value of resilience

It was going to be a tough annual general meeting (AGM). Two profit warnings, the numbers down and the minority shareholders needed their dividend. The finance director was going to come under particular fire. The view of the chairman, Brent, was that the board and the management team had done a good job. The company needed restructuring and this had been carried out diligently. The company would soon be back in profit, but not in time for the AGM.

The chairman spelt out, step by step, the nature of the company's performance, what had needed to be done and what was required for the future. His eloquence and clear thinking went down well. But one shareholder could not control his impatience. He interrupted the chairman with one difficult question after another, and each question included a subtle insult directed at the chairman or the CEO, sometimes both. The other few disgruntled shareholders took heart. The AGM could have spun out of control. However, each time the chairman was interrupted, he stopped and addressed each critic in the same calm manner he displayed at the start. He listened, commented, listened again and commented more. Even when the demand was made for him to resign, the chairman addressed that point in the same measured way as all other points raised. He drew on evidence and made a clear case that he was the best man for the job, but that this needed to be reviewed at the next AGM. The institutional shareholders had so far been quiet but were increasingly impressed by the inviting and yet no-nonsense manner of the chairman. To them, he soaked up pressure. For them, this was the man for the job, especially as the further restructuring that was about to take place would put the board and the management team under even greater strain.

'This is the man and the team for the job. I trust it will put this company right', concluded one of the largest institutional shareholders. What the chairman recommended was accepted by a significant majority. After the meeting, the single most vociferous minority shareholder said to the chairman, 'You did it again! How?'

'It's all part of being chairman. It is my job to convince the shareholders that I can steer this company through the next demanding phase. They need to have confidence in me. They needed to know I can keep this boat afloat.'

The vociferous shareholder knew this to be true. A calm, pleasant, sociable exterior camouflaged an inner core of steel. Although the shareholder would never openly agree with the chairman, he held a quiet respect for the man and in many ways knew that his was the chairmanship demanded by the situation.

Inner strength

Resilience – the capacity to cope with stress and avoid catastrophe – is becoming a critical skill in an increasingly stressful and demanding world where debilitating mental illness and burnout have become one of the leading threats to organizational achievement and productivity. Resilience relates to the ability to respond well to adversity, which could apply to a wide range of challenging events, from the trivial and annoying to the truly tragic. Individuals who perform don't always have the highest IQ, but have an inner strength to work their way through all of the daily stresses and strains as though they are a completely ordinary experience. For the high-performing manager, pressure is just one of the challenges to be faced.

Resilient people avoid asking, 'Why me?' and instead ask, 'What now?' Someone with a high RQ doesn't waste time looking for individuals or events to blame; instead, they look for causes and effects so that they can grow personally and help others avoid or hang tough through similar circumstances. If you develop a high RQ, you will almost always find the good in every situation you face.

A key aspect of resilience is the individual's ability to understand and empathize with others. Resilient people demonstrate emotional intelligence and exhibit a high level of self and social awareness along with an ability to effectively manage themselves and their relationships with others, especially under strain.

Some say that we 'bounce back' from adversity, and that only minor setbacks allow us such a rapid and complete recovery. Major, life-altering challenges change us in such a way that we don't return to the point we were at before being confronted by them. Instead we slowly 'come back' from life-altering experiences in a painful manner which engages all of our resources to face, endure, overcome and – hopefully – emerge transformed by the experience.

A sensitive character with a clever brain can be highly vulnerable because they may falter and question why such a situation is happening and ask themselves how they can withstand it. This in turn generates more data and increased pressure. Because they are clever, an overly complicated self-analysis can lead to an even quicker spiral out of control. Rather than simply reacting to change, resilient people actively engage in it. They believe in having the capacity and responsibility to determine their own destiny rather than feeling powerless in a specific situation. Inner calm is needed to display an external appearance of calm. The benefit of this is that people believe you can see through and beyond oncoming adversities. This allows a focus on expanding influence through assertive behaviour and actions and preparing for change, no matter how traumatic it may prove to be.

High RQ gives the individual the emotional capacity to survive work without falling apart under intense pressure. You must understand yourself, the situation you are in and the challenges that have to be faced. This is vital given the normality of senior roles, which often involves a continual stream of political strife.

Inside resilience

A lot of research has been carried out on the subject of resilience at work, but there are also many gaps in knowledge as to how exactly possessing a greater or lesser degree of resilience, or RQ, is directly responsible for how individuals manage complexity.

Most of the resilience work on record has been taken from military sources, in particular the US armed forces, on how troops can be made tougher, both at the organizational and the individual level. To date most of the thinking has focused on individuals, so there is a growing need translate the principals of resilience over an entire institution.

The existing research on resilience in terms of corporations and departments has been scarce, and one of the reasons behind this is that for all intents and purposes, resilience is just a word. As a concept it covers many other aspects of the 5Qs, but when all of these different elements are combined, it comes out as a uniquely different hypothesis.

Resilience is not a clean concept; rather, it is a result. So what exactly is resilience? Basically, it is the ability to work through and survive a distinctly stretching experience as well as have the capacity to face adversities. So resilience is two things: an ability to survive setback and adversity. Adversity is a continuous experience; a setback is a singular event. Can you survive setbacks? Can you work through adversity?

As Steven Snyder comments in his *Harvard Business Review* article 'Why Is Resilience So Hard?' (2013), 'Despite the overwhelming consensus and supporting evidence that resilience is vital for success in today's business environment, the truth remains: resilience is hard. It requires the courage to confront painful realities, the faith that there will be a solution when one isn't immediately evident, and the tenacity to carry on despite a nagging gut feeling that the situation is hopeless.'

Americans have fundamentally accepted these two elements and come up with research that says it is a deep skill, that what you need to do in response is 'X, Y and Z'. In other words, in the same way you train a soldier, you can also make the organization work well. Our experience is that it is actually this, plus something else.

Mission-based leaders have an advantage when it comes to resilience. By definition they are focused on delivering value – which requires them to engage with their stakeholders. It promotes a culture of challenging and questioning, which nurtures a culture of resilience. In mission-based organizations, people are encouraged to speak truth to power (to use Al Gore's phrase). It is an evidence-based culture where leadership assumptions are tested in the crucible of practice. This encourages inner strength as opposed to creating dependency of others on the leaders so that no opposition emerges. Vision-based leaders, in contrast, can become isolated and adopt a bunker mentality when reality starts to diverge from their vision.

If we consider organizations like the John Lewis Partnership, Caterpillar and the Omani government, what do they all have in common? The answer is a deep-seated set of values that are lived on a day-to-day basis.

The John Lewis Partnership has a deep-seated value of service; its mission is to deliver exceptional service. Caterpillar embodies the value of quality – again, this is its mission. The Omani government harbours an ingrained value of happiness. It is only the second nation in the world with a prime objective being the happiness of its citizens. Brunei was the first nation, and Singapore tried but gave up, even though they were better organized than many others. This tells you that resilience is not a skill; rather, there is something incredibly deep in the psyche and philosophy of all those people who are running the country or the organization.

The chairman of the John Lewis Partnership is central to the organization. John Lewis has no CEO but two managing directors, who head up Waitrose (the food business) and the John Lewis stores.

The John Lewis governance structure of employee ownership requires the chairman to act as sensitive steward. All this is to ensure that service and respect for people remain the core elements of the enterprise. The embodiment of these values lies in the fact that for many years John Lewis won more tribunal hearings over staff grievances than the complainant staff. Even though John Lewis is rarely taken to tribunal, very few UK organizations can boast such a record.

In the John Lewis Partnership, the value of service goes back to 1920 when service was a critical factor. The founder, John Lewis himself, said that service was a critical issue, and that he was the one person who stood out after World War I when people were basically trying to survive. He said that although enhanced customer service was expensive, it was a primary issue.

For Caterpillar in 1914, C. L. Best and the Holt Manufacturing Company, who had joined forces at the time of the Great Depression when starvation was taking place in the Midwest of the United States, held to a mission which said they were going to make money not from agriculture but by selling tractors. At the same time, these tractors had to be of such high quality that Best actually sold what few possessions his family had just to eat, so that he could make the finest first tractor to sell. These sacrifices ultimately paid off.

So what are the values of your organization? This is question number one. When you see an organization where one value statement quickly follows another, you know one thing: its values are finance and consequently meaningless.

The reaction of individuals to such supposed values is distaste, dislike, negativity and ultimately some form of demotivation. Vacuous values kill loyalty. This same loyalty is not dead in the John

Lewis Partnership, and the moment you walk into a branch of other retailers, it is possible to witness the differences between the two. One way in which John Lewis retains its values is that everybody across the organization lives them – so training and development for middle and senior management around those values results in very practical outcomes. It is a fundamental process that all staff are trained in the John Lewis Partnership. There is no holding back on training, just as in Caterpillar.

It is difficult to locate any dearth of individual loyalties within Caterpillar, primarily because they don't like bringing search consultants or other resources in. Instead, they prefer growing and developing people from within the organization itself.

What is on display as a result are individuals who not only possess genuine values but also are training to live them. These values further determine economic benefit. The John Lewis Partnership chairman is the lowest-paid chair of any of the largest companies in the UK. He is paid less than many GMs who are competitors. Why does he do this? Because when he is seen to be sharing the same experiences of the staff on the bottom rung of the organization, then there is a sense of family, built on the realization that managers make the same sacrifices for the company that they ask their colleagues to make.

What happened at Caterpillar, one of the largest companies in the world, is clearly possible for all organizations, should they choose to follow such a worthy and indeed worthwhile path. In Caterpillar, suits and dressing smartly are required for public meetings, but otherwise the normal attire for top management, including the CEO, are the same yellow overalls that all of the workers wear. If you visit the second biggest office of Caterpillar in the world, in Singapore, you will find the CO and all of his colleagues wearing yellow, showing that everyone is connected and supporting each other. People there also recognize that the individual's pay is comparable to theirs, with salaries and budgets based on an emotional, rather than an industry-wide expected, ratio. This is not a completely mathematical process, but it works.

There's something deeply comforting about the idea that a superior isn't being made a multimillionaire out of your hard work, but there is more the concept of 'This is my leader, they work hard, I can see this, they don't drive a Rolls Royce, they're a normal sort of person, they have a bigger house than mine, but that's OK because I respect them.'

Talking to Ed Rapp, one of the former top executives of Caterpillar, it was clear how the company sustained their values even when pressurized to pursue short-term outcomes. Top management lived the values of the firm through their adherence to due process, emphasizing transparency and the equitable treatment of all. Frequent consultations with staff are part of living in Caterpillar. Their mission to continually enhance quality does not refer to just products or services but to all aspects of Caterpillar life. It is rare that dramatic statements are made about being the biggest or the best, but instead more subtle comments concerning 'I wish to leave my office in a better state than I found on my entry' are made.

The number one point with resilience is values, and these values are deep because they have been in place a long time. The key question from the organization is to look at their value statements over the past forty years and see how they have changed. Now explain what values you really have, because if you go over the statements of the John Lewis Partnership, or Caterpillar, or Federal Express, they haven't changed.

Why fix something that isn't broken? Values determine economic reality, not the other way around – this is step one to resilience.

Whose job is creating resilience?

It always must be the chairperson, CEO or, in the case of a country, the head of state or their equivalent who creates resilience. Following this, it needs to be established who has the role of defining and gathering the evidence which will prove central to creating and reinforcing a resilient climate.

On coming to power, Sultan Qaboos bin Said of Oman gave citizen well-being immediate priority. Inequalities were minimized and the values of care and concern for each other pronounced. He lived these values himself, as did his ministers. By following this path, Sultan Qaboos made one of the more serious public statements of any leader in the world. Most people could see that their life was good. They could witness such critical values in practise.

It is rare for any nation to have no riots, but under the stewardship of Sultan Qaboos this is the case in Oman. What he did differently was to look at the overall situation and speak with all members of society and all of the relevant key institutional stakeholders, including women's and family groups. Following this, he said, 'Yes, this is the line to take.' The process worked due to the high level of engagement with the citizens.

Sultan Qaboos then went further: he redefined the purpose of the nation so that Oman could survive after his rule was over. To achieve this, he brought in a series of advisers whose task was to break down 'happiness' and translate the concept into an economic reality that would benefit the citizenry. This has proved important and means that Omanis, once trained and qualified, don't have to go abroad because they can't find a job at home. It has also served to give pensions to families and rights to women. In particular, important areas of the economy such as tourism and fishing resources were identified so that they could receive appropriate investment and flourish.

Sultan Qaboos of Oman did something that only one other prime minister, Margaret Thatcher, has ever done. He brought together the senior public servants and the CEOs of the top companies and trained them in the strategy of working together and pursuing well-being as the nation's primary goal. Many people may be surprised that Thatcher had an interest in engraining sharing and understanding into workplace. In 1986, she called for the initiation of the Top Management Programme, which did exactly this, allowing business and government people to review the strategies for the nation whilst also being developed as leaders of the nation. It is testament to Thatcher that some of these original groups still meet to this very day.

Thatcher helped develop a set of values about why the market should be equally available to everyone, by giving shares to the ordinary workingman. Sultan Qaboos enacted a similar process in Oman. Rather than focusing on the marketplace, he stressed the importance of community, a fact which some CEOs didn't appreciate because they felt it would take attention away from realizing profitability. However, they bought into it! They knew that Sultan Qaboos was right. He epitomizes these values, and is genuinely concerned about diversity and the well-being of citizens in society. Diversity is normally forced upon individuals rather than them actively embracing it.

Sultan Qaboos decided that there was no particular ministry that should be targeted, but rather that all of his ministers in the Cabinet needed to work to improve the happiness and resilience of Oman's citizens. Other than Thatcher, it is difficult to recall a prime minister telling their Cabinet that 'whatever else your job is, you will all do this as well'.

Never knowingly undersold

The values on display in Oman and within organizations such as the John Lewis Partnership demonstrate a palpable level of care and concern for others. Six months after the 9/11 attacks, there was panic that London was going to be the next terrorist target, and the one store thought most likely to be hit was John Lewis at the intersection of Marble Arch and Oxford Street. This fear became so extreme that for the very first time there was serious conversation at John Lewis that it would have to close and make staff redundant, a proposal that went against everything the business believed in. John Lewis's chairman at the time had a background with the Foreign Office, but he also had the values of John Lewis running through his core. It would be unlikely that he would work in the Foreign Office today, given the global political climate at present. His was a community-based philosophy, and he effectively said, 'OK, let's put our values to the test. We are going to have economic reality versus our values and, if everyone as a community feels strongly enough about this, we will test it.'

He held an internal referendum that was a choice between option 'A', you will all receive your bonuses and any other additional payments owed, but we will have to close this John Lewis store, or option 'B', no bonuses for anyone, but the John Lewis store stays open. Everybody has to pay for the store's future. If you are working at John Lewis in Carlisle, where there is high unemployment and you are possibly the only person working in the family, or are a mother who's not paid very much to begin with but is also one of the then 56,000 shareholders in John Lewis, for you not to get your bonus this year is a big deal, not a luxury. The eventual result was well over 90 per cent in favour of option B. An overwhelming majority effectively stated, 'I will forego any personal gain because these are our people and we won't let them go.

This illustrates that there are examples of values working so deeply that they actually determine reality. This is why, if you want to be resilient, you have to cope in a way that mirrors the John Lewis Partnership approach to managing adversity. Oman now has the potential to become a country that is significantly different to anywhere else in the world. This isn't the result of a few clever people skilfully carrying out a single task. Rather, it is based on a set of deep-seated values that are absent in most organizations. In fact, the only track record for many companies that refer to values is a reference to their founders.

The deterioration of original values is one of the most common factors uniting many corporations today. When Cadburys Schweppes separated, all of the values which originated with their founder disappeared as well. Barclays Bank was originally touted as 'the people's bank', but today many perceive it as being singularly concerned with shareholder value at the expense of its customers. It sacked its chief, Antony Jenkins, actively and publicly in an attempt to bring back the bank's core values, in large part because he was not generating enough profit.

Going from short-term transactional reality to deep-rooted values is very difficult, and it is clear that most organizations today are not resilient. They do not have a transformational mindset based on a total community. Instead, they follow a transactional mindset, focused on the economic value of each asset the organization possesses. BHS is a classic example of how a company that was founded as being for the community, its staff and customers was totally destroyed by the greed of just two men. At the same time, Sports Direct's operational conditions have been criticized as being worse than Victorian workhouses in many cases.

As Rosabeth Moss Kanter explains in a *Harvard Business Review* article (2013), 'Resilience is the ability to recover from fumbles or outright mistakes and bounce back. But flexibility alone is not enough. You have to learn from your errors. Those with resilience build on the cornerstones of confidence – accountability (taking responsibility and showing remorse), collaboration (supporting others in reaching a common goal), and initiative (focusing on positive steps and improvements). These factors underpin the resilience of people, teams, and organizations that can stumble but resume winning.'

The number one issue required to address all of these complaints is values. Number two is education. The Margaret Thatcher story was based on education, because she recognized that public servants needed to understand competitive advantage, and that the private sector could not continue as it was until it fully understood public policy in all of its ramifications.

Organizations that are resilient invest heavily in education, even when things are going badly for them. This could work in terms of developing internal concepts, or as public policy. Education systems are most likely to succeed when they take the form of 'concept plus leisure', for example, the process of developing people over the long term. This can be explained by the mantra 'We don't hire the best for this transaction, we develop our own people to cope. If we need external experts, we will bring them in only if it becomes absolutely necessary.'

There is an inherent distaste in organizations such as the John Lewis Partnership, Caterpillar and Federal Express for search consultants. The latter may successfully identify an external person for an important role, but within months this individual is likely to find themselves isolated because, more often than not, they lack crucial understanding of organizational culture and choose instead to champion a simplistic, transactional profit approach that cannot deliver for a wide array of stakeholders.

One of the UK's top civil servants emphasized his enthusiasm about engaging the stakeholders. His challenge was to hit targets on behalf of the community and at the same time meet government demands for cutting costs. The challenge for the Civil Service is embedding effective stakeholder management, whilst living up to their values of service, professionalism and equity.

There is a breath of fresh air behind this new-look Civil Service and what it is trying to achieve. One of the first questions asked is, 'How do we educate our public servants now that we have lost the Civil Service College?' The different needs to consider are, How expensive will a new college be? What level of sophistication is required? Which experts are needed to advise the review? Which civil servants shall we develop? The emerging thinking is that leadership development is central to effective Civil Service functioning, bearing in mind the challenges to be faced in delivering a service that thrives on diversity.

Reality and RQ

The final element of RQ is the need to be realistic.

RQ has to be evidence based so that the consequences of change can be measured and understood. It is of course possible to become overwhelmed with the volume of potential evidence, but the entire purpose of this process is to bring everyone onto the same page. If the organization is open and honest about what it is doing and how it will be done, and the evidence is shared with the board, management and staff, then everyone understands what is happening and believes it is true. As a result, everybody becomes realistic.

What happens if this evidence is tainted, one-sided or only emphasizes the CEO's point of view? Then the results only serve to demotivate and generate high levels of mistrust. People cannot be realistic and begin to feel that mistrust and demotivation are holding them back. However, this need not be the case. It is the fact that they do not know what they are meant to be doing that halts their progress. It is the lack of realism, which leads to opposing somebody who represents the way forward, which ultimately results in both sides finding fault in each other's arguments and ultimately cancelling each other out.

Despite this, top management will continue to force something through because they say they are being opposed by people who are behaving unreasonably. Ironically, this is probably true at this precise point. However, the reason they are being unreasonable is that the bosses are being irrational in the first place and there is no common ground to make either party realistic. This is where evidence becomes crucial.

What evidence should be gathered? Data should capture evidence trends, specific business issues or investments details, but the most powerful evidence is how the organization is currently 'living'. What and where are the system blockages or fault lines? At which point are the values of the organization not being adhered to, actively rejected or promoted? Much of this will be soft evidence and has to be coupled with hard data, such as 'If we buy this how much will it cost?' or 'If we do that, what will be the outcome in terms of profit?' Evidence gathering has many phases. It includes collecting knowledge as to what is going right and wrong, along with significant interviewing and testing. Hard data may initially seem more attractive as it displays so-called facts.

When soft evidence has consequences built into it, gathering up the data takes longer. 'We have to get your opinion if we do this as to what the consequences will be.' One opinion will be slightly different from another, in which case we have to aggregate this information, meaning that soft evidence gathering is an expensive and time-consuming initiative. The ultimate challenge posed by this process is that the organization is often left feeling slow and lacking in the necessary resilience to face up to its challenges. In fact, the opposite is true. By taking its time in collecting evidence that involves consequences, and digesting this information more carefully, the organization actually becomes more resilient.

This is because fundamentally people say to themselves, 'If circumstances dictate that I have no clever strategy for getting a bonus at John Lewis in the months immediately following 9/11, then at least I can understand and accept the situation.' Because they fully appreciate the situation, they can prepare and make changes to their personal budgets, not changes to the organization. Quick evidence, in contrast, focuses only upon the transactions an organization is committed to, and the consequences are based singularly on this detail. This results in a 'We want to do this, and if this is the case, then these people will have to go because otherwise it blocks our plans.' The bigger, long-term plans and effects are lost for simplicity's sake.

Taking all of this into account, we can confidently state that resilience building is based on values and education that require time for soft evidence to be accumulated and properly evaluated. Organizations which lack resilience often rely on hard evidence that, on the surface, appears to be quick to gather and of great resulting value. However, more often than not, it is no more than adequate preparation for failure.

RQ + IQ

IQ runs through all of the Q's. For example, with MQ it is important to put up an argument based on and supported by an ethical stance. With PQ, how can you be a successful political player without having a cohesive argument? Otherwise, you will be viewed as just another untrustworthy loudmouth. With RQ, the argument is, 'We become resilient by taking over 300 managers and walking and talking with them for at least two weeks, not by jumping in and expecting them to run.'

IQ is systematic preparation of the organization for any eventuality. Resilience comes from knowing all about the organization's issues, potential and flaws. The managers understand the consequences, so they can see the alternatives. When there is no apparent alternative, it becomes clear to them that they must all pull together, which is partly an emotional process but with a very rational outcome. When you work closely together with others, it becomes a highly emotional practise. There is little or no emotion left when you are trying to put together an argument that you know is essentially wrong.

The *régler*

In the area of resilience, academic literature refers to the *régler* – French parlance for someone who constantly adjusts. So if there is a problem, we will 'adjust' the budgets, or the target, or anything else which will lead to eventual success, rather than look at the bigger picture or problem.

On the day following the UK referendum to leave the European Union (EU), the public were being told by the EU that their budget and economic plans were finished. By law, the UK would be entitled to complete its budget allocations for Europe until the day it exited the EU, but officials and naysayers said this would not happen. This meant that anyone whose work depended on close links with Brussels would be cut out of their existing networks and there would no way for them to connect with their Continental counterparts.

Would the UK government really accept this state of affairs? No, of course not. Instead, they will continue to give the exact same amount of funding they currently contribute for all of the years ahead, so organizations and individuals can continue to interact with their networks and complete projects as usual.

The *régler* response of 'fix it for today' works on the assumption that such an arrangement will continue into the future indefinitely, without considering the long-term cultural damage caused to values and practises that is taking place. This outcome occurs when organizations avoid dealing in evidence and pretend to have firm values which are simply not reflected in their everyday activities. When it comes to resilience and the *régler* – the one who switches, adjusts and repeatedly changes course – they will tell you that everything is great, but actually nothing has changed.

The term *régler* is the antithesis of resilience.

Action points

RQ is a must at the very top of an organization. The ability to handle difficult and demanding circumstances is a leadership requirement today. It is about surviving but surviving well, and displaying strength of character that people can admire.

Assessing your leadership RQ:

- What and who are your emotional and physical supports?

- Where can you look for additional support? Are there people in your life whom you know you can rely on?

- What are the balancing factors in your life – the activities and relationships that maintain your physical and psychological fitness?

- Where will you find the emotional strength to see it through?

5

MQ: Competitive advantage through moral decision-making

Jim was head of the Asia Operation. In the eyes of many at the meeting, he was the next CEO. The topic of concern was a regional country and one of its company's targeted for acquisition. The mood of the meeting was in favour of purchasing the country's organization, but Jim disagreed.

'We are a company of strong values. We believe in our mission and that is quality! The question is, will our sense of quality be badly impacted if we go into this country with this particular business?' He had answered his own question. 'It will. No one dare say it, but it will. The fact is we will be forced to offer bribes.' Everyone at the meeting knew this to be true. 'Yes, we have to go to this country but not this way. We need to work with a prospective partner who is flexible enough for us to renegotiate contracts and establish a new culture, new values and reward system that will prevent bribery from taking place and allow quality to shine. This will take time.'

There was still a question no one dared ask.

'I think I know the one question that is on your minds: how will our shareholders react when they find out that we may not go through with the acquisition, and that we are likely to lose out on a $3 billion revenue stream for the next few years? Yet, my response to the shareholders is simple. We do not compromise on our values. The fact that the price of our shares is high is down to us living the values of quality we espouse. We should not be reluctant to proclaim that we live quality in all that we do.'

Jim swayed the meeting in favour of voting against the acquisition. Most of those present felt that a drop in share price would follow, despite the fact that they all knew Jim was doing the right thing.

Doing the right thing

Ethics is discussed a great deal in management today, sometimes glibly. 'The ethical company', 'ethical manager', 'engaged leader' and 'role modelling' are all terms, which have become common in the business vernacular. Our final quotient is MQ, the ethics and moral factor. This produced some surprising results in our research.

Fred Kiel, an expert in the field, addressed the issue of MQ in his book *Moral Intelligence 2.0*. He shows that leaders with high MQ provide a greater return to shareholders than leaders with less MQ.

According to Kiel, moral intelligence means having the ability to lead with integrity, responsibility, forgiveness and compassion. Integrity yields trust; responsibility inspires; forgiveness promotes innovation; and compassion breeds organizational loyalty.

Yet in recent years we have witnessed a string of corporate scandals leading to the collapse of – or huge reputational damage to – major organizations. Think of the banking industry during the financial crisis or Volkswagen's emissions scandal. In many cases these organizations were headed by leaders who were intellectually intelligent (IQ), people oriented (EQ) and politically smart (PQ). Yet despite this, they failed to deliver sustainable value. This can, in part, be attributed to a lack of moral intelligence.

Passion, humility, energy, the ability to deal with adversity and a desire to do your best at all times are the minimum MQ requirements for those who aspire to lead. Employees watch and learn from their leaders, and when role models set a bad example, you can expect those who follow to mimic such behaviour.

There are many leaders on Wall Street and in other financial centres, as well as in government organizations around the world, with a demonstrably low level of MQ. Bernie Madoff, for instance, was no doubt a smart man, a smooth talker and an expert at navigating a landscape of regulators, investors and journalists over the course of several decades. However, his lack of moral intelligence ultimately revealed the unsustainable foundation of his empire.

The checking function offered by MQ should not be seen as a restraint but rather as an asset that allows managers to focus on the long-term credibility or success of an organization, sometimes at the expense of short-term gains. In our example, Jim held such a focus. Without a moral perspective, the peaks and troughs of governing will continue to produce ill-conceived policies. The failure of social, political and business leadership leading up to the financial crisis reminds us of the urgent need to revise current leadership models for both business and government organizations.

MQ has two components. First, you as a person: your good intentions and values. Second, the demands of the situation you find yourself in. Good leaders are invariably associated with ethical leadership. Ethical leaders put the needs of their followers before their own, and also exemplify private virtues, such as courage and honesty, while exercising leadership in the interests of the common good.

Unethical leaders do none of these things, but bad leadership can be corrected if action is consciously and deliberately taken. Morality at work translates into applied ethics, which includes limiting tenure; sharing power; resisting self-aggrandizing hubris; staying in touch with reality; retaining a sensible work–life balance; remembering the organization's purpose; staying healthy; being creative; and setting aside regular time for contemplation.

Leaders can also improve their implementation of MQ by establishing and fostering a culture of openness. This can be demonstrated by taking action to appoint an intermediary, such as an ombudsman; encouraging the placement of strong independent advisers; circulating reliable and complete information; and establishing a system of transparent checks and balances. When unethical behaviour is uncovered, the outcomes quickly result in a loss of investor trust, irrevocably tarnished reputations, unwelcome regulation, public demands for legislation, enhanced training and the introduction of independent directors.

Sometimes these outcomes are not the result of intentionally bad people. Why? Because of the situation. No matter how ethically well intentioned staff and management are, the reality of operating in international governance regimes means having to address tough decisions, which differ considerably from everyday personal dilemmas. For example, what should you do in a country when bribery is the way to do business? The immediate instinct is not to bribe, and yet not doing so can have repercussions that may include a substantial loss of income, a drop in share price, the loss of markets and possibly 5,000 people at home being made redundant. Doing the right thing often has a high cost. Therefore, in today's world of increasing inequality and ever-increasing government corruption, senior managers face a series of unwelcome dilemmas. There is no easy way through this, and so it has become commonplace for leaders to try and muddle through as best they can.

'There but for the grace of God, go I', observed a senior banker we spoke to. He was confidentially discussing the activities of his bank prior to the global financial crisis of 2008: 'Yes, we knew that many of these financial instruments were risky, but everybody was flooding the market with them and we were all making money. After a while that felt normal, even though all of us knew that what we were doing was screwing investors and ordinary people who were using their life savings to provide an income for their future.'

You are what you believe

In many ways MQ is as fundamental as IQ. The very essence of life is captured in our ethics, our morals, and how they are formed and guided by those around us.

One of our contacts was an executive at a tobacco company. He was managing director, despite believing that the sale of tobacco was immoral. The trade-off for him was that the money was good, that he could send his children to private school, that he could give his family the life they wanted – even though his wife disapproved of what he did for a living.

And it wasn't just the product that made his life ethically uncomfortable. Anyone who works in the tobacco industry is likely to routinely encounter bribery. Our contact was no exception. When meeting some Middle Eastern government representatives, he habitually handed over bribes. Often he didn't know when he went to a meeting with a minister whether he was going to be arrested. One of his competitors had actually bribed one minister twice – once to get a deal and a second time to lock up the competitor.

Bribery feeds on itself. The tobacco executive found that you bribe a little, then you bribe a little bit more, and then you have to bribe people in that network a little bit more, and after a while that becomes normal. And, while this was going on, he was doing well and was one of the best managing directors in the company.

Eventually, he felt that his own morality was becoming clouded and he left. Though his income was severely reduced, he has been happier ever since.

The tobacco executive faced an ethical dilemma, as do many managers. The reason for that is sheer complexity. Fundamentally, our organizations are getting bigger, so there is no one single way forward. Inequality in the world is getting more pronounced, and governments around the world are corrupt. These two factors – inequality and government corruption – drive corrupt practise.

Ethics in its original sense was not a matter of right or wrong. The term 'ethics' is derived from the Greek word *ethos*, which actually means 'custom' or 'usage.' It does not mean not what is right or what is wrong, but what is done and what is not done. The original foundation of ethics was not a moral position; rather, it was simply behaviour that was more accepted. What we have done, particularly in the West, is take a moral position, viewing ethics as right and wrong. Other traditions from around the world, from Hinduism to the Chinese approaches to philosophy, have done much the same and thus miss one critical imperative, which explains why good people continue to do bad things.

Which line to draw?

It is easy to think that MQ is simply about knowing where to draw the line. When does accepting a gift from a customer or supplier constitute cultural sensitivity and good manners, and when does it constitute a bribe? When is employing a family member good talent management, and when is it nepotism?

How we understand what is and is not ethical has implications for how leaders behave. Our views of morality are shaped by our perception of what it means to be ethical. Put another way, it would be a lot easier to do the right thing if it were clear what the right thing was. Instead, managers often face a moral maze. This is partly due to differences in moral philosophies.

There are many different ethical positions that come from moral philosophy, but there are three that stand out.

Deontology (or deontological ethics) focuses on the rightness or wrongness of actions themselves, as opposed to the rightness or wrongness of the consequences of those actions (consequentialism) or to the character and habits of the actor (virtue ethics)

The great German philosopher Immanuel Kant was a champion of the deontological theory of ethics. According to Kant, certain universal principles dominate the whole of life, and these stand above the demands of context, circumstances, families and individuals. So Kant promoted the notion of absolute virtue. Deontological philosophy denotes a deep moral sense and requires considerable strength of character in order for a person to fulfil his or her duties. Under deontological philosophy, it is impossible for the ends to justify the means, for the only right and moral way forward is to do what is right. Even if nobody wins at least the right actions were taken.

Deontological ethics is about being black and white. So, for example, it is the belief that killing someone is morally wrong regardless of the circumstances. Similarly, it is always wrong to steal.

Teleology (or teleological ethics), however, takes a different line. Under teleological philosophy, the ends justify the means, especially if the community is to benefit. The greatest good for the greatest number was the original moral position in ancient Athens, and it underpins the ideas of the English philosopher Jeremy Bentham. In other words, there is no ultimate right or wrong, so we have to try to understand what is best for us in these circumstances.

Teleology, then, is a theory of morality that derives duty or moral obligation from what is good or desirable as an end to be achieved.

Utilitarian-type theories hold that the end consists in an experience or feeling, namely the ends justify the means. So in teleological ethics it is morally acceptable to kill someone in self-defence, or for a father to steal to feed his children.

With a deontologist, the question is not just 'What is the right thing to do?' but also 'What is the right way of doing it?' With a teleologist, there may be a right thing to do, but we have to be conscious of all those people around us. So our way of doing something may be immoral but the intention may be totally moral.

The third moral philosophy, relativism or moral realism (or moral objectivism), argues that there are moral facts and moral values, and that these are objective and independent of our perception of them or our beliefs, feelings or other attitudes towards them.

Practicing moral relativism involves adjusting to the moral code of each context. That is, 'when in Rome do as the Romans do'. Relativism is the ultimate contextualist position, which means you will change your moral philosophy according to where you are at a particular time. In the business world today, teleology and deontology dominate; they often coexist in an awkward double standard. Relativism is more obvious in terms of culture. So most of us adjust to different cultural norms of behaviour, including what we wear, eat, drink and so on when we travel or live in another country, but we probably don't alter our ethical stance.

Certainly, there are very few managers and corporations today that have actually taken on a relativist position by declaring that in Nigeria we bribe – and it is absolutely right – and that we are going to be quite open about it and do it much better than anyone else.

Navigating the moral maze

From the point of view of practicing MQ, then, there are three different moral boundaries that the manager can draw: the one that is absolutely black and white (deontological); the one that seeks the greatest good (teleological); or relativism.

Between these philosophies are inherent tensions and contradictions.

The paradox that faces top management is, 'I'm judged deontologically, but I have to trade teleologically. And in order to get that done, I need to behave according to relativism'. And there's no way out of that. The message is all three moral positions are running concurrently. That gives rise to the awkward double standard referred to earlier.

So the governance requirements are, for example, you don't bribe, you don't bully and so on. But what do you do when you're operating in countries where such practices are widespread? The answer is that behaviour varies with context.

So we find with MQ that there is no consistency within organizations. They may use very fancy MQ words, but the practice is vastly different because of liberty and because of leadership.

Today most of us are driven by consequences. How would you feel if you found a child in your family, whom you dearly love, stealing? How would you see them? Would you see them as morally wrong, or would you see them as a child in trouble, who actually needs your help and guidance now more than ever before? If the latter, then the one thing that you would do is keep them away from the police because you know that this child is vulnerable. You know that your fundamental moral philosophy in the family would never have allowed them to get to this point unless they were desperate, so the conclusion is this is a child in severe difficulty, and if you put more strain on them, you risk pushing them into a position that is irreversible.

The reality today is that most companies – unless they are in Asia – are not in growth markets. Most of the rest of the world is now dealing with saturated markets. The MQ consequence is that your products and services no longer provide the key competitive advantage unless you have a very innovative technology. This means that a key source of competitive advantage is the manner in which you trade, the respect that you have established, the reputation that you have to defend. So MQ is increasingly important, having moved from being a way of doing things to actually being a consideration for competitive advantage.

And yet how do companies behave? They say, make money, cut costs, outsource *and* be moral.

Notice each of those words is 'and', 'and' and 'and'. Yet these imperatives may be – and often are – in conflict with one another.

We have seen this with Volkswagen and its emissions testing scandal. We may see it again with investigations into other car companies. Do we really believe that only VW cheated on its emissions? Do we really believe that the engineers and senior managers at all the other car companies were so much smarter than those at VW? The one reason why nobody dares speak up about anybody else is that they were all in the same boat, and so morally the car industry, just like the finance industry, is actually teleological: it is driven by consequences.

As our markets today have become saturated, they are increasingly motivated by consequences. So what are the big ethical dilemmas that we face today?

The reality is that business is driven by leaders who follow the teleological philosophy, because if they didn't, they couldn't do their job. How can you establish relationships with other chairpersons and CEOs in other countries, ministers of state and so on that you have to have for those big company contracts unless you share their teleological philosophy yourself?

How could you hope to win a $10 billion contract in a country of different governance to your own to extract zinc if the moment you walk into the room, you say it is wrong to bribe? Bribery in certain countries is standard practise. And so your company having a deontological CEO means you create discomfort. That person may be absolutely right, but in a teleological world, a deontological person automatically creates differences.

What are the big ethical issues facing companies today? The first internal issue is a culture that encourages bullying. The irony is that many of the individuals who do bullying think they are doing the right thing. I've got to achieve my targets, they reason, so I need to be tough. I've got to meet these objectives, so I need to be disciplined. The manner in which that shows itself is by being unsympathetic to others. Yet the question remains, when does being disciplined become bullying?

It is true that as a leader you may have to drive through a context that is holding the company back. You may have to introduce sweeping changes or introduce cost cutting. But why do you have to harass the people you work with? Why do you have to bully them? And why is that practice allowed to continue until it becomes a norm? You reach a point where bullying and harassment is at its highest when nobody dares speak up. People are suffering, and the managers who are doing the bullying actually think they are morally right.

This phenomenon is highlighted in Al Gore's latest book, *An Inconvenient Sequel: Truth to Power*. Many companies face the same problem – those in power intimidate the people beneath them and silence their opposition. In the political sphere, this is evident in the extreme leadership styles of Donald Trump and Vladimir Putin.

The problem is that in many companies people are so afraid to speak up that the powerful leaders operate as bullies without ever questioning their own behaviour.

Why does the bullying continue? From an ethical point of view, the answer is the power of relativism. Take another extreme case of the German serial killer nurse Nils Högel. Högel was sentenced to life imprisonment for the murder of six patients, and has now confessed to killing thirty patients. In 2017, a police investigation concluded that he was probably responsible for at least ninety deaths.

German police are now investigating how many of Högel's colleagues knew what was going on without raising their concerns.

Why do good people do bad things?

Clearly, the example above is extreme, but it points to a culture of silence that people are unwilling to break even when lives are at risk.

In business, it is more likely that jobs or money is at stake. But these can have the same result. The moral paradox is most pronounced at the top of the organization, at the senior leadership level.

The point here is that all three moral positions run concurrently: you are judged deontologically; you have to consider the greater good teleologically; and yet you have to behave according to relativist pressures. In reality, there is a dynamic relationship between the three positions that senior managers (and all of us) have to navigate. Many of the people who behave unethically are browbeaten into doing bad things.

Different attitudes towards bribery, for example, create an ethical hall of mirrors – and a moral maze. In some African and South American countries such as Nigeria and Venezuela, bribery is the norm. So to get on in these places, you are obliged to adopt the same attitudes and practices.

Our research suggests that companies that don't bribe in these sorts of countries are usually start-ups. In one case, the CEO of a start-up energy company in South Africa received several unpleasant midnight visits from the African National Congress. But he refused to participate in any sort of corruption. He appointed a very good team and they were successful. The problem was that as the business grew, the company had to sustain itself by covering its costs and making a profit. This meant that it was dealing with multiple-level agencies – national government, regional governments and local governments. The managers were inevitably browbeaten into bribery.

Bribery seems to occur when a company has grown beyond a particular size – when it reaches the M side of SME (small to medium-sized enterprise). The reason is that it is dealing with government, and government in many parts of the world is corrupt, and life in the local communities is unequal, with high levels of poverty and so on. So what do you do?

Our research found different types of behaviour at different levels in the organization. The GMs, the country head or the regional head typically meant what they said. In the majority of cases, their moral orientation was to be good corporate citizens. In other words, they put the greater good of the company first (following a teleological morality). But this may not be matched by the ethical stance of the top team.

In extreme cases, the top team may effectively hang the GMs out to dry. One German company we encountered, for example, was in the resources business trading in South America, so they were dealing with countries such as Colombia and Venezuela. The company was building roads and dealing with extractive products. A new CEO was appointed in Germany who said there was to be no more bribery. But the economic structure of the company meant that 85 to 90 per cent of the profits in South America came from bribery. So it had become a standard practice. It wasn't regarded as bribery anymore; instead, it was marketing.

The new CEO insisted that any of the GMs or country heads caught bribing would get no financial or legal support. So for being good corporate citizens and putting the interests of the company first, the country managers were now likely to go to go to prison. The GMs didn't know what to do, so they complained to an external consultant who knew the company culture well. They also appealed to the company secretary, who was a very decent individual. Faced with a situation where the moral need to meet performance targets led to immoral behaviour, the corporate secretary didn't know how to square the circle. Which morality were managers meant to actually pursue?

The company secretary felt that the company should either decide that managers didn't bribe and accept that it would miss its targets, or continue to operate as it had done in the past. What was morally unacceptable, he believed, was to deliberately put the GMs at risk. Not knowing what to advise them, he resigned.

And so the GMs felt themselves to be even more at risk. The external consultant knew the newly appointed CEO, so had a candid talk with him. After a long conversation, the CEO admitted that he knew that bribery was a standard practice, and that the company couldn't function without it. The consultant asked, Why are you doing what you're doing, when you know that this is an inherent part of the business? If it's so bad and you feel it's wrong, why don't you sell the company? But the CEO said the business was too profitable and he would not consider selling it.

He admitted that reputation and increased press attention were going to be an important strategic factor under his leadership, and that he was prepared to sacrifice his GMs, breaking a culture of trust. It was a commodity business, he reasoned, and the GMs were a commodity. The consultant was shocked, but the CEO argued that even if two or three of them went to prison, and another two or three resigned, he could bring in new GMs who would stay for four or five years.

So the question is, who was behaving immorally? The GMs, who were doing the best they could and were taking personal risks? Or the CEO, who was content to treat his GMs as expendable units?

Eventually the company was taken over, the CEO was fired, and it's now bribing even more under the umbrella of another company.

These sorts of double standards are not as rare as you might think. The example above highlights the impossible position managers can find themselves in – even those with high MQs. In fact, we found that the ones who hold the highest level of moral orientation were the GMs. This is because they are the ones directly exposed to the markets, and they are the ones who had to display acceptable (moral) behaviour within the company.

GMs need to demonstrate high MQ because they are the ones who are really doing the job. The challenge of making the strategy work falls to them rather than the top team. Often this means some very difficult ethical juggling.

Mission impossible

One GM we spoke to described his ethical position as 'mission impossible'. This is where the link between MQ and RQ is most apparent. It takes a great deal of resilience to make sense of the ethical dilemmas that GMs routinely face, and even more resilience to draw the ethical lines.

You need a lot of RQ to be an effective GM, and especially if you have a high MQ and seek to change the ethical climate you operate in. In the few cases where we found examples of a company trying to change local conditions, the GM – sometimes without the permission or support of head office – always led it.

One manager was based in Singapore, and the company was operating in Vietnam and the Philippines. He was determined that there was to be no more bribery – and he achieved his goal without sacrificing his operational managers. It took about three years, which is typical of attempts to eradicate bribery. The reason for this is that there is another moral imperative: the people contracted to the company through the supply chain. The company has a responsibility to them, and many of them are small businesses and don't know what else to do. So you're trying to change a culture whilst you're also trying to meet the moral obligation of keeping people in employment and not damaging the local economy even further.

The view that a company can simply stop bribing is simplistic and has immense moral and economic consequences in local markets. The GM in Singapore decided to tackle the issue head-on because he noticed that the people most at risk were not the company's employees but the local suppliers. Often the last thing the person running a 50 to 100-person business wants is a culture of bribery. They hate it. They don't want to pay extra. They just want a normal Western life.

To bribe or not to bribe

Morality or ethics are principles that demonstrate right and wrong behaviours. One of the big ethical issues today is bribery, which now appears to be at its highest levels ever. From our confidential coaching discussions with GMs and C-suite executives, we estimate that around 80 per cent of Western corporations bribe regularly on at least a monthly basis. This is, of course, well hidden within the supply chain through multiple agency relationships.

One common interpretation of ethics is the adoption of a moralist perspective by using set protocols and interpretations of right and wrong ways for resolving dilemmas. This approach is inherently judgemental.

The contextualist viewpoint is different. It is up to you to find ways through uncomfortable and even immovable moral challenges. Imagine your company has been caught in the act of bribing. The offending executives are removed. Culture and ethical programmes are put in place for all relevant staff and management. Change is brought about, and the reputation of the company improves. However, nothing has altered in the country where bribery took place. So, what to do next? Only when leaders champion and personally consistently demonstrate ethical standards and behaviour, can corporate governance hold any real meaning in an organization.

There is often a sense of tangible amazement when directors linked to bribery escape any real prosecution along with extortionate termination pay-offs, while organizations do their best to ignore threats from the public to no longer buy services or products in protest against unethical practise. Organizations need people who are able to distinguish between behaving rightly and wrongly, and have the courage of their convictions. From our experience, the vast majority of leaders know what is right and wrong, but how they act is a different matter. Leaders are waking up to the reality that the world is a complex and demanding place, and that the assumptions of what it takes to be a successful leader are now very different compared to the past.

The principles of moral intelligence – integrity, responsibility, compassion and care – cannot be established on a part-time basis.

A leader's behaviour, responses to others' mistakes and reaction to disappointments offer revealing insights into the character of the leader and the true values of an organization. Trust takes time to build and, when breached, relationships are altered and can prove difficult to rebuild. This is why MQ matters.

Unethical behaviour can only be challenged when leaders develop functional expertise and organizational knowledge. They should invest in building soft skills and learn how best to work and empathize with others. Ethics is a philosophical term that reflects the character of an individual and an organization, in the latter instance conveying a meaning of moral integrity and consistent application of values of service to the public. It represents what is morally accepted as 'good' and 'right' in specific environments. The challenge of what constitutes ethical behaviour lies in a grey zone, where clear-cut decisions and outcomes do not always exist.

The concept of ethics is intimately linked to that of values and enduring beliefs, which influence the choices leaders make. While some values – wealth, success – have little direct connection with ethics, others – such as fairness and honesty – are concerned with what is right and so can be described as ethical values.

The critical link between ethics and values is that ethical standards and principles can, and are, applied to the resolution of value conflicts and dilemmas. What is clear is that these conflicts, dilemmas and continued misalignments are now greater and are becoming more apparent than ever before. Why? As stated throughout this chapter, it has become a matter of increasing complexity due to ever-larger organizations; the intermingling of politics and strategy, community and business; and a desperation to meet shareholder and stakeholder demands. So, what can be done, especially when these dilemmas are exposed and in the public eye?

Business versus moral imperatives

One of the interesting things about MQ is the way we treat morality today. You've got to be good at business, you've got to cut costs, you've got to make a profit and, by the way, could you also be moral? Something has to give. What is lacking in most businesses (and is still not being taught in most business schools, by the way) is the need to establish a moral position which determines how you deal with costs, how you deal with profit, how you deal with job losses and other human costs. This requires a deep philosophy that is a moral philosophy at an organizational level and is fundamental to the culture that drives the place.

And yet if you look at how we are dealing with our institutions, we are not dealing with them in that way. We are dealing with them as a series of requirements: make profit, cut costs, outsource and be moral, almost as a series of techniques or tools. No wonder we find masses of ethical dilemmas – because we are mistreating what MQ is.

We are not treating the moral dimensions with the same respect we are treating the other Qs. It really is as simple as that.

One of the reasons why we condone immoral actions is, we don't know how to deal with moral actions. If we did, we would not make our organizations hostages of profit, forcing managers to cut costs, outsource and be unethical. Instead, we would put a moral code first and allow that to determine the other decisions and their consequences.

Thinking short and thinking long

Our research found that GMs typically did what they said. The GMs of the highest moral standing not only try to preserve their internal culture but also try to change their external culture. Often they did so was despite being under (unspoken) pressure not to do so because it could upset the presence of the company in that country. And often head office was more concerned about how the national government would react to a reform taking place at the local level.

That was not always the case when it came to the top team. There was a lot of rhetoric about behaving morally, and internally, inside the company, that was pursued to varying degrees. Externally, though, it was less so. For the top team, share price was one of the most sacred issues to defend. Allowing any circumstance that undermined competitive advantage could affect share price.

This means that when it comes to MQ, in many cases, GMs are thinking more long term than senior managers. The top team is thinking about the immediate effect on share price. And the board, which is concerned with governance, is thinking even more short term.

Governance basically falls into two categories: the compliance side, which is what most boards look after, and the stewardship side, which is the oversight and which determines the real moral tone of the company.

The board is the only body that can address or work through cultural issues with the CEO and the top team. In earlier research by the authors, this phrase emerged: The management owns the strategy but the board owns the culture.

That requires stewardship, and stewardship requires finding out what's really happening in the field. So you may need to visit Nigeria or South Africa to find out what's going on, and most board members know that. If there's a reluctance to practice stewardship, that can have a knock-on effect on the sustainability of the company long term, irrespective of whatever's happening in developing countries, including bribery. The lack of stewardship often means that cultural issues inside the company are not addressed because the CEO in particular and members of the top team are given licence to operate the way they want. By not drawing those moral boundaries, however, the senior management team is storing up trouble for later

Vision-based versus mission-based leadership

Senior managers are in a difficult position when it comes to moral dilemmas. So what can they do to mitigate the tensions and help their GMs?

The first step is to acknowledge the complexity that exists and the ethical dilemmas it can create. This requires a lot of attention and the building of trust internally, but just having a discussion can make a big difference.

Where we found companies had done something to address these issues, they had one feature in common. It was not just the moral orientation of the leaders, but rather it was the fact that the company was mission oriented. So, for example, companies such as the John Lewis Partnership and Caterpillar handle the moral dimensions of their business more directly and have a better long-term approach. For them, being the biggest, the best, the most powerful, the most dominant in the market is not the issue. They live on the value they create and the values they adhere to

So John Lewis values service, and Caterpillar values quality. And those values determine strategic actions. Therefore if the company is going to make a lot of profit but service is going to be undermined, John Lewis will not pursue that strategy, even if it means not opening a new store. And that has been one of the main reasons why its supermarket chain, Waitrose, has been limited to very particular markets. Waitrose will not go abroad because they're concerned that service will not be satisfactory.

Similarly, on a number of occasions when Caterpillar has been stretched, the company has refrained from going into a new market because quality might be compromised. In the early days in China, for example, because the company could not control what was happening there, especially when dealing with the government, it was cautious about expanding and came under tremendous pressure from shareholders and the media. But the board and the management would not shift their position. The company is in China now, but it has invested heavily to treat China much as it would the United States.

The difference here is between mission-based companies and vision-based companies, and we have referred to such difference at various points in this book. Vision-based companies, which are often the vision of one person or a small group, are companies that are most vulnerable to ethical weaknesses. This is because the true values are not the values of the company, and the moral boundaries are not clearly and consistently drawn.

In previous research[1] involving interviews with managers in over eighty organizations, we found that only 18 per cent of organizations actually had a true mission base. And that had nothing to do with geography. The most outstanding companies in the most difficult conditions actually provided superb conditions for their employees in that context. In one case, a company in China run by Chinese, not Westerners, had eliminated all forms of corruption. And right up the street, another company might be bribing, exploiting people and so on.

So the mission-based orientation is very much reliant on the original founding values base of the enterprise. Caterpillar was started in 1917, and because of its original values, the company survived the 1930s when it was selling tractors during the Great Depression. Its values are much the same today.

So the first point is to acknowledge the ethical difficulties and tensions that doing business in different markets and parts of the world creates.

Second, it is important to establish and sustain a culture that allows an ethical conversation to take place. This is because, fundamentally, when you have a conversation about, say, bribery, you're acknowledging that it's happening and by implication you're giving permission for it to happen. And that's breaking the law. So having that conversation is difficult. But some companies manage it.

The third way forward is to ask whether you are mission based or vision based, and what it takes to have values that can be fully

[1]Andrew Kakabadse, *The Success Formula: How Smart Leaders Deliver Outstanding Value* (London: Bloomsbury, 2016).

integrated with the organization's economic thinking and economic criteria.

The alternative is that you are willing to continue sacrificing your GMs to a double standard. We were at a company conference – the top 250 or so leaders, including the top team, board and general management. The CEO stood up and said, 'We don't bribe anymore' – and the whole place burst into laughter. Even the CEO had to smile and laugh a little bit himself (but not too obviously), as did the board members.

And everybody clapped for him. So just for confirmation's sake, we asked. 'Why are you clapping?' And one manager said, 'This is the best joke of this year.'

The reality in this company, and in a great many other companies, is that the senior management is trying to manage an impossible paradox by giving tacit approval to a double standard. And they're doing it quite well. But the more and the better they do it, the more the local context suffers, and the more the inequality and deprivation that occur increase. In the short term, the company survives, and makes a profit. But the long-term damage and reputational risk are immense.

The ultimate way forward has to be moral reflection by the top executives. Many would hold the view that they can be both deontological and teleological. In other words, 'I can do the right thing and I can be morally flexible.' But in fact, throughout the centuries, that's the one thing it's been shown that people can't do. This is amoral. You can't say, I am black and white, and then turn a blind eye. Nor can you turn a blind eye until you are found out and then hang your people out to dry.

So when that conversation takes place, the immediate ramification that wakes people up is everybody else can see what you're doing. You're saying you're black and white with everybody else – except yourself, your friends, your family, your inner circle. And that damages trust badly.

That raises the question of authenticity. Being deontological with the rest of the organization, but teleological with yourself and your inner circle, is the one best way to ensure that you're seen as inauthentic. And that is how you're dealt with. Everything is fine to your face, but nobody really trusts you.

So when that self-confrontation takes place, improvements usually follow. And the real question becomes, how am I going to draw a moral boundary versus what economic losses am I going to accept?

Without a considered and honest debate about the moral dimension of business, the corporate scandals will not be stemmed, the reputation and status of business leaders will continue to fall and the harm to peoples' lives – the victims inside and outside corporations – will perpetuate.

Action points

MQ research shows that moral consciousness is a must for today's leaders. We need to trust our leaders, be they in politics or business.

Assessing your leadership MQ:

- Trust is now very visible because of social media and other forms of communication. How will you manage that transparency?

- Managers now face more dilemmas than ever before – and many of those dilemmas aren't of their own making. This means that each leader's moral consciousness is now a vital issue, which it probably wasn't even ten years ago. The problem is that there are three very different moral perspectives you can take. Often those three run concurrently with each other. Which of the three moral positions (right and wrong, greatest good for the greatest number or 'when in Rome') do you subscribe to? Where will you find your moral compass?

- Clarity is all-important. Coming to terms with what your line is and being realistic about it is vital. There is nothing wrong with admitting to yourself that your real moral driver is the greatest good for the greatest number, so there will be casualties, for example; or 'when in Rome, do as the Romans do', which means you may be criticized for changing your position from one context to the next. The important thing is to be clear. Can you bring that sort of objectivity and clarity to your decision-making?

- As a leader you are a moral role model for people who are younger or lower down the organization. What do you want to show them?

- Because your clarity is visible two things emerge. First, even when you are being inauthentic, other people may still trust you because you are being honest. Second, how you act could actually improve the situation, so people will have sympathy. Do you have the stomach for making hard decisions?

6

The 5Qs at work

In the first five chapters we examined the 5Qs and explored why they are the capabilities required of leaders. This final chapter provides an overview of how the 5Qs work across different work domains – levels in the organization – and the transition between work domains.

Specifically, it explores which of the Qs is most relevant for the four leadership work domains: operational management, general management, strategic leadership (top team) and governance leadership (board level).

The four work domains

The first work domain is the operational management level responsible for delivery – that's typically middle and junior management.

Second, is general management, which is where strategy and execution meet. It is a very sensitive meeting point – and it's a fracture point. This is where things often go wrong.

The third leadership work domain is strategic leadership, which is the top team, the executive leadership of the organization.

The fourth leadership work domain is oversight, or governance, leadership, which is the board.

We observed which of the Qs are used more than others in these four leadership work domains.

In organization after organization and industry after industry, the rules of leadership are changing, and if you don't have all 5Qs, you may well be left behind. Many of our long-held beliefs and assumptions are simply out of date.

In mature markets, it is very difficult to measure or maintain a competitive advantage. It's a constant challenge to engage with your audiences and stakeholders, and come up with compelling propositions. So what attributes does a leader need in such a market?

The need for cognitive intelligence (IQ) is well documented, and nobody would argue with the assertion that a leader needs to be able to harness resources, particularly where there are multiple agendas. An advanced emotional intelligence (EQ) is clearly needed to develop teams to achieve their potential, through managing your own emotions as well as those of others within your team. But as we have seen in earlier chapters there are other qualities that are needed as well.

Political intelligence (PQ) is a leader's ability to navigate a way forward through diverse stakeholders' agendas. And resilience quotient (RQ) is absolutely necessary to cope with the pressures imposed by today's complex business environment; it determines how self-aware you are, and how able you are to deal with negotiations and survive across multiple contexts.

Finally, a moral quotient (MQ) is becoming increasingly important, which means taking an ethical approach to the way you lead. But in many markets, especially in less-developed countries, a combination of inequality and corrupt governments has seen incidences of bribery reaching epidemic proportions, and it is increasingly difficult for middle management, in particular, to impose their emotional and moral intelligence. They are often stuck in the middle, facing an impossible task of satisfying both senior management and their clients without succumbing to a delegitimized supply chain. Ultimately, such scenarios are unsustainable, as they deliver less value.

The 5Qs come together to inform every aspect of leadership, and each of them can, in different ways, be nurtured and practised through learning and development. The world is constantly changing, and our model of what makes a great leader therefore has to be continually reviewed and refined. But from what the current research tells us, a balance of the Five Qs appears to be the foundation for an effective and sustainable approach to leadership.

Senior managers, CEOs, chairs and government leaders increasingly work in complex, technology-rich, fast-paced environments and economies, struggling to deal with previously non-existent challenges. Contemporary governance calls for a varied and versatile cognitive approach to problems, and this problem-solving framework should be based on the 5Qs

When harnessed and utilized in a balanced fashion, these intelligences provide an individual with the sort of holistic and dynamic mindset that is capable of analysing and addressing the world's problems.

A recent study on effective transformational leadership in the public sector sheds light on the nature, interrelationship and relative importance of these intelligences. It found that high-performing leaders simultaneously employ the five key leadership intelligences to achieve effective transformational change. Much like DNA's constituent nucleic acids create the substance that works as the framework for human life, these 5Qs come together to inform every aspect of leadership.

The study tested this concept on elite leaders (ministers, undersecretaries and C-level executives) in the United Kingdom, Australia and the Gulf region. It was applied on four critical levels of leadership according to work domains: Delivery (operational); General Management; Strategic; and Governance.

These four work domains reflect different clusters of work practices, ranging from relatively simple tasks and activities that require rational thinking and teamwork at the "delivery" level, through to the complex positioning of concepts and subtle influencing of stakeholders at the "governance" level. Think of a visa processor in the Ministry of Foreign Affairs in the former case, and the foreign minister himself/herself in the latter. Leaders working at different levels and in separate work domains require different combinations of the 5Qs.

Our research highlights that the 5Qs are not consistently practised across these four management levels. The larger bold lettering shows high usage. The smaller text illustrates more minimal usage (see Figure 1).

Variations in the combination of intelligences required in each work domain reflect differences in the nature of the challenges confronting the leaders. These combinations change according to seniority and the strategic and operational considerations faced.

While a high level of IQ appears necessary at each level, the degree to which leaders are required to utilize their PQ increases as they rise through the organizational hierarchy. In contrast, leaders draw

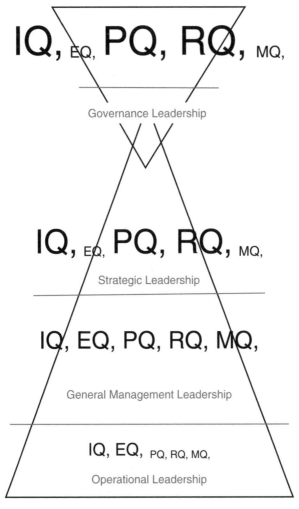

FIGURE 1. *The 5Qs in Action: A Bottom to Top Analysis*

most on their EQ at the General Management level, and less so at the Strategic and Governance levels.

High-performing strategic leaders possess the ability to analyse and skilfully handle conflicting agendas, for example between IQ and PQ. Being a team player is important but not critical at this level. In government especially, a high degree of PQ and EQ allows civil servants to best understand the interests and reactions of all the involved parties – the most important being the citizenry. It is incumbent upon both the minister and the civil servant to find ways through conflicting demands and to emerge with a viable policy and provide services for the public. The citizen may not know what is the right policy, but they can quickly sense when they are not being well served.

Looking at this more closely, we have already suggested that IQ, EQ and PQ are 'value free' intelligences. A leader with high cognitive, emotional and political quotients can apply these for good or bad purposes. Moral intelligence, however, is by definition 'value led' and provides a checking function or a conscience in decision-making. It is odd to report that the higher one moves in the organization, the less ethical and moral the practices become, irrespective of what is said publicly. (This controversial point is discussed in more detail in Chapter 5.)

The failure of social, political and business leadership preceding the financial crisis reminds us of the urgent need to revise current leadership models for both business and government organizations.

While one can debate whether IQ is inherited or developed over time, the evidence suggests that EQ, PQ and MQ can all be cultivated through a life or career. A leadership model emphasizing the nurturing of these intelligences is timely and will fill serious gaps by instilling in the next generation a balanced and informed mental framework for addressing policy problems.

In a world where the political, social and economic landscape changes rapidly and without warning, all leaders – particularly in the public sector – must possess the fundamental building blocks to achieve sustainable results.

Operational leadership

In the operational leadership domain, it's fundamentally IQ and EQ that make the biggest contribution. Operational leaders need to build teams, they need to build authenticity, they need to understand each other and they need to be open. To be an effective operational leader, you also have to be smart with good IQ.

The other three Qs – RQ, PQ and MQ – are not used so much in the operational role. Operational leaders are not put under the same sort of strategic pressures as top management, so resilience (RQ) is less important. You don't really have the same moral boundaries to draw. You don't really need to play politics unless you're playing them at a personal level. These three Qs become much more critical when you transition to the next leadership work domain – general management.

General management

In general management, all of the Qs are used all of the time because you are at the point where strategy creation meets strategy execution. GMs are often not directly involved in the strategy creation, but they're the ones who know which strategies will work because they're the ones who truly understand the context of the markets in which they operate. The GMs are in many ways the pivot upon which the organizational strategy lever works or fails.

The GM role therefore is absolutely critical to the success of the corporate strategy. But being a GM can also be a thankless task. At times they have to convey a message upstairs that things are not going to work, even though they're being told, 'Make it work.' At the same time, they have to convey a message lower down that this is going to be the way forward, even though everyone knows and tells them, 'You know it's not going to work, so why are you asking us to do this?'

Making the transition from operational to general management is one of the most challenging (and underestimated) career changes. The need for EQ – being open, being authentic, understanding each other's emotions – is coupled with PQ, an awareness of all the sensitivities that are part of the EQ you use, but you use PQ in pursuing your own agenda.

So how do you do that? The IQ part, which allows you to understand the strategy execution arguments and how you convince people to follow, stretches you because even if you don't quite believe the argument that you're putting forward, you still have to make it compelling. The phrase 'caught between a rock and a hard place' could have been coined for the GM.

The resilience (RQ) you need to cope is also high, because you're caught between two levels of management – operational and strategic – and the MQ part is the most moral side of management, because you're pinched between the realities and the rules. Nobody else can face those except the GMs.

Many of them try to behave in the most honourable way – and that typically means behaving honourably towards the corporation. Whatever else they may be forced to do in the markets or local communities, at least they are the genuine servant of the company and they're doing the best they can, irrespective of the pressures they are under.

Strategic leadership

When you get to the strategic leadership domain (top team), the first thing to note is that the concept of the team doesn't apply. The irony is that there isn't a team in the top team. Rather it is a group of leaders who come together in an arena where competing interests are negotiated. So the EQ requirement drops, because this is not a team; rather, this is a meeting point of interests where you're trying to find a way through and engage with a number of misalignments and tensions. The biggest misalignment at top team level is competitive advantage. If you are the senior manager looking after Asia and China, your view of competitive advantage is likely to be very different to your counterpart managing North America.

But the top team has to come up with a comprehensive view of competitive advantage for the organization's stakeholders – the markets, the shareholders and lower-level management. So life at the top constantly involves dealing with misalignments and engaging through them, when there is no easy way forward. So the IQ part increases even more when you transition into the strategic leadership work domain, but you have to put forward a compelling argument to support your case when there are good arguments against you. The EQ component drops away completely because you can't be open under those circumstances. But the PQ element increases dramatically because what you're doing is pursuing your agenda in the way that you genuinely feel is the best way forward – and which has consequences for the organization.

Living in this world of misalignment puts the leader under pressure, so the RQ part is one of the most important dimensions of strategic leadership. It's tough at the top, and especially in the top team, so you need to be resilient to cope. The statistics on depression and the resilience of individual managers bear this out. In the City of London, a medical analysis was undertaken concerning the mental health of directors across banks, financial services and insurance companies. It found that 22 per cent of this population were under active medical treatment for depression.[1] That was just what was visible – who knows how severe the problem is underneath the surface.

So there is a personal consequence to living in a world where you're constantly juggling ways forward when the markets are changing and you have colleagues who are convinced that their view is right. Often, too, their views are evidence based and correct for their part of the business. But two views together, drawing on different evidences, don't come up with a shared conclusion. They come up with a shared tension.

How do you deal with that? What we've witnessed with many senior managers is that they try to minimize conflict to reduce tension. Tension in this sense is good – it's a difference between us

---

[1] Author interview with medical practitioner.

that we can talk about. It shows how we're thinking – and it shows the experiences that we have in our roles as, say, the marketing director or the finance director versus any other director. And at least there's evidence that we can talk about and come to some conclusion about. So there has to be some sort of compromise.

The real problems begin when the tension spills into conflict and the lines are drawn. The best way forward with conflict is to deal with it offline. So at a board level, it means the chairperson has a private discussion with one or two board members. It means the CEO has a private discussion with one or two of his or her directors. And it may mean the departure of one or two directors, and that is not because they aren't good at their jobs but because they are in conflict with another leader. You may be excellent at your job, but the organization cannot function with a very powerful and competent individual drawing on evidence in a clever way and disrupting the team even more.

So, at the strategy level, it's not a team; rather, it's a group. It's a meeting point of interests. The challenge in this strategic leadership work domain is coming up with a cohesive way forward when there are different perspectives on competitive advantage. That is the skill. And that explains a lot of the MQ verbiage and low practice. MQ at this level is less about the moral imperative and much more about being seen as doing the best that can be done under the circumstances.

Governance leadership

Much the same happens with the transition to the governance leadership domain, which includes executive and non-executive directors and CEOs, except that the IQ component is even higher than before, because you're now publicly exposed as the board. There are two points to make here.

The first concerns the executive directors – CEOs and finance directors in particular. Because they are full-timers, executive directors have additional insights and knowledge about the company, which the non-executive directors do not possess. But like the non-executives (independent) directors, the executive directors are required to stand above their executive role and provide independent oversight and opinion even about projects they may have initiated or may be closely involved with. If they do not demonstrate the oversight role, how can the non-executive directors trust them, and especially the data they feed the board?

The company secretary, who is the key point of information and the individual closest to the chairperson, but is still in an executive role, provides the other key executive oversight role. The company secretary is likely to be the board member who is the first to know the nature of forthcoming challenges. How such sensitivities are then facilitated – with governance and stewardship concerns uppermost in their minds while they are also being judged on their performance by other executive directors such as the CEO, the legal counsel and the finance director – creates a special tension on the board.

The second point applies to non-executive directors. Non-executives have the same legal responsibilities as executive directors, but have less knowledge about what's really going on. You're just a part-timer. The question is how can you have the same insights as a full-time executive director?

So now your arguments had better be good, especially as the chairperson. The idea that the board is a team is again a complete misnomer. A board is a meeting place of interests, and these interests should be made public. So it is the place or arena that is the safety valve for the organization. The moment you become too much of a team, you lose independence. So the big issue with a board is, how do you maintain independence and at the same time have a meaningful conversation? The answer is that it's very difficult.

One German director observed, 'A big difference between a German board and a British board is that we Germans are too honest to be polite, but the Brits are too polite to be honest. So how do you actually talk?'

His point is partly borne out by what we've found with boards. The political skills are now even more vital than at strategic top team level, because you have to spend a lot of time away from the board meeting forming relationships and discussing issues. In fact, most non-executive board members have a portfolio of directorships. So it's not a full-time job. They have a number of jobs across a number of companies.

Where those political skills, used at their best by the way, run into problems is when the board member has too many board memberships. So his or her portfolio is too big. Our research suggests that the maximum number of directorships an individual can perform effectively at any one time is three, or possibly four, depending on their responsibilities – in addition to one chairperson role and one non-executive directorship.

One country that has sought to enforce this through its stock exchange is Australia. The Australian stock exchange published lists of directors it calculated held an inappropriate number of non-executive directorships, and it deemed them unable to fulfil their stewardship oversight responsibilities.

Stewardship is the critical issue with boards. It takes time to understand the company; it takes time to understand your colleagues. You've got to work through all those difficult issues, and you must have the time for it. The danger in what we're doing in many countries is making boards overcompliant and under-representative in oversight and stewardship.

Contrary to public opinion, it could be argued that we're not paying board members enough when you consider that the complexities they're dealing with are much greater than ever before. And in many ways they have no choice but to be political in the most positive sense, to have a very sharp mind that puts forward a compelling argument and to be resilient, because unlike management, they don't quite know as a board member when a scandal is going to break. You may have an inkling, but you don't know in the way that management often knows when a scandal is going to arise. So you could be attending somebody else's board and all of a sudden there's a radio announcement that you and your colleagues on another board are now going to be under scrutiny because something went wrong.

So the resilience needs to be much higher, and that's why in many ways the practice of MQ at the board level is the lowest of all of the four work domains. It's just an impossible situation where you're trying to juggle share price, perception and belief in competitive advantage, with the reality of the markets in which the organization operates.

The conclusion we have reached after many years of observation and research is that really good board members are exceptional individuals because it goes with the job that they will be judged unfairly. And there's no way around that. Essentially you're trying to handle each and every concern. It's not a crisis yet; rather, it's a concern, and you have to navigate your way through those concerns context by context. So your ears had better be close to the ground. If you are the chairperson, you better have created a culture of board members visiting sites, trying to understand management and building a relationship with management but at the same time having that culture of independence.

When you lose that culture of independence, that's when things go wrong. But keeping that culture of independence alive also means that you have a responsibility for stewardship. That's a tough task when you're faced with the challenge of maintaining share price and profitability. It can be even tougher when you may be operating in South America, Eastern Europe and beyond and Africa, where there may be corruption in the system, but you need the system to continue functioning. That's why there is tension between MQ, PQ and IQ.

Managing tensions

The role of the strategic (top team) leader and governance (board) leader in most international organizations is fraught with ambiguity and conflicts.

The only exception we have observed is at top team and board level in mission-based companies.

So there is a difference between 80 or so per cent of the world's companies, which are vision based, and the other 20 per cent, which are mission based. The distinction is fundamentally that mission is based on values, while vision is based on economic criteria. As we saw in the previous chapter, mission-based organizations provide a more favourable environment and leadership context.

In these organizations the MQ is high but the EQ is low. So at the top team and board level it's still not a team. It's still a meeting place of interests, but there is a moral boundary that's built into the fabric of the company.

The other takeaway is how you transition between the four leadership work domains. What does it take to move from one work domain to the other?

Transitioning

Transition 1: We found that in moving from operational management leadership to general management leadership, the fallout rate of very bright people, MBAs and so on, was about 34 per cent. That should set alarm bells ringing in any organization that believes in effective talent management.

What was the critical factor that made the difference? The politics. The leaders who didn't make a successful transition could not handle the disruptive nature of relationships with constant negotiation and the unrelenting pressure. It actually offended their lifestyle, their home life.

So what does it take to go from operational leadership to general management leadership? It's first an understanding of what it means to be a GM and the exposure that you have. Second, it's coming to terms with what it means to trade and do business in the part of the world you're in. So if you're regional manager Asia, that's what it means.

Third, it's learning how to negotiate with head office. And you'd better be good at that. What many people – some of the most intelligent people – find, is that intellectually they can do the job. It's the resilience to do it day in and day out that they struggle with. They don't have that capacity. And that's why there is such a high fallout rate.

Transition 2: Transitioning from general management to the top team is another big shift. It means coming to terms with the fact that the top team is not a team but a group of interests. Most GMs have been used to creating teams around them and below them, and creating a collegial atmosphere across the organization (or at least trying to).

But functioning at the top team level means fighting for your budgets. It is coming to terms with the fact that this is a meeting point of interests, and that your interests should predominate over anybody else's. This is the case particularly if you have an aggressive CEO who's not a good team player him or herself.

It's then coming to terms with the fact that share price and reputation are based on perceptions which are more important than the reality of what you're doing in various markets or communities. We talked to many GMs who said, 'I totally understand the job, I totally understand the pressure the top team is under. I admire them for that, but do you know something? It's not for me. I don't want that lifestyle. I don't want to take home these problems to my family. I'm very happy with the money I've got. I really don't want those types of pressures. But intellectually I can handle them.'

And that's what we've found. Intellectually, they can handle them. But they don't want the other pressures.

Transition 3: Transitioning from top team to board requires the ability to transition from management to stewardship – and from hierarchical control to personal influencing. With many directors, controlling things is an issue. In the board role they find they have no hierarchical power, so they have to exert an influence through personal relationships. Having to keep a distance from the company in order to ensure compliance and independence is difficult.

Some of the worst chairmen we've encountered are actually former CEOs. And some of the best chairmen are experienced at organizations where hierarchical control is not the norm. So they are senior partners from professional services firms such as McKinsey or KPMG. Mike Rake at EasyJet, for example, brought in Carolyn McCall from The Guardian Media Group and she made a tremendously positive impact at EasyJet. Mike Rake was a senior partner at KPMG.

So the key capabilities include knowing how to facilitate a way forward, often with impossible challenges to overcome. Knowing that you're exposed to a legal environment, which is unforgiving but yet you have to create a culture and trust externally in markets that are difficult to operate in, is a challenge in itself. Coming up with a compelling argument is critical. Thus, the IQ element is even higher than before. The PQ part is even higher than before. And then the resilience to cope when you have no levers of control needs to be higher than before.

So one thing we've found at the top team and the board level, strategic leadership and governance leadership, is there is a difference between feeling authentic and being seen as authentic. We've come across many top people who actually feel themselves to be authentic, but who have done one or two things that are certainly not authentic. And they are seen as inauthentic by others in the organization, but still feel themselves to be. And the reason for that is, they have genuinely done the best they can do under the most difficult circumstances. What most people don't see is how much worse the situation could be, but the top team leader and the board member can see that.

So authenticity actually means something different at those very senior levels, and that in itself is something that's difficult to come to terms with. And for many GMs, something they don't want is recognizing that they're going to work in a world, and walk into a world, where they'll feel themselves authentic, yet will be seen as inauthentic and not receive the respect of their colleagues or the people around them.

Most of the issues that derail leaders, once they've gone into general management and above, have nothing to do with their brains, their abilities or their experience. Most people are good. The issue is often the emotional side, the resilience. It's how their colleagues see them – the reputational loss that they may face. It's the pressures they don't like. It's the lifestyle that they want.

One thing is absolutely clear: when you get to the top level, it takes exceptional character to survive in that world.

There's a sense in the literature that CEOs and senior managers need to be psychopathic. We haven't found that.

We've found people who are highly focused, people who are doing difficult things, people who have to push forward. And when you dig underneath the surface and get to know them, they're highly vulnerable individuals who are suffering for what they are trying to achieve and have a lifestyle that is not all that pleasant and that you wouldn't wish on anybody.

But the perception of their focus, push and drive makes them seem like the stereotypical psychopath, when actually they're people who need help. Leadership is probably the toughest job in the world. Perhaps its time we acknowledged that – and offered the people who do it more support and sympathy. That's not about paying them more money; instead, it's about paying them the respect they deserve.

As a society we need leaders. Many of us are not equipped or prepared to fulfil that role. Leaders – real leaders – have to make difficult judgements and decisions with imperfect information and under time pressure. Sometimes the lesser evil is the best outcome we can hope for. We understand that in the political sphere, but are still playing catch up in the business sphere.

Greater understanding and appreciation of the difficult job that senior managers do – and the importance of the five Qs – would go a long way towards creating a new leadership model based on the realities of the different leadership roles and helping talented managers make the necessary transitions. That has to be in everyone's best interest. We hope this book can go some way towards furthering that debate.

Action points

The 5Qs are not applied in the same way throughout the organization. The reason for that is complexity. The moment you leave behind an operational leadership role and move into more strategic and governance type circumstances, it is difficult to handle those complexities because there are no clear answers.

Assessing your leadership for all 5Qs:

- Leaders have to navigate through transitions. The biggest of these is the step from operational management to general management – you will be stretched more than at any other time in your leadership journey because the evidence shows that you need to deploy all 5Qs at the same time. That means being open and honest with your EQ as well as political in using PQ, and at times undermining yourself due to the moral circumstances that exist but that are not your fault. Are you prepared for these trade-offs? How will you manage that?

- GMs are probably the group that's most at risk of burnout or derailment. Having the breadth of mind to make the transition from operational to general management is a big challenge. Is that a challenge you want to take on? What will it mean for your family and other relationships?

- The biggest challenge for a GM transitioning into strategic leadership lies in two areas: loyalty and what it means to be a team. At the top, you are trying to get the best out of the assets at your disposal, which means loyalty to people is only one concern and may have to be sacrificed. At general management it is the principal concern. Are you willing and able to make that transition? Can you put the best interests of the organization above the people who work for it?

- At the top, the leader is not part of a team as such; rather, it's a meeting of interests. How you approach that depends on how you see the best way to position the assets to achieve the optimal results. Your sense of team is challenged at senior management levels. Can you make that adjustment? Can you be an effective advocate for your part of the organization and fight for your corner, whilst also being prepared to make sacrifices and horse-trade for the good of the business overall?

- With the transition from strategic management to a governance role, the big change is that you are far more exposed. The management team might get away with something, but the board is expected to act if it perceives any wrongdoing. Are you ready for that responsibility?

- Moral issues are more prominent at the governance level, yet you have no authority other than exerting an influence. This means that the way you make your arguments and put your case together has to be even better than before. How will you ensure you have the right information to build your argument?

APPENDIX
The 5Qs Checklist

Instructions

Read how you behave in the following 14 scenarios. For each scenario, you are given five alternative behaviours. Please rank these behaviours in order – with 5 as the most likely for you to adopt and 1 as the least likely for you to adopt – in the box provided. In preparing your ranking, visualize yourself in these scenarios and be as honest as you can in your responses.

Scenario 1: At meetings

At meetings, which of these behaviours are you most likely to use:

1. rational arguments leading to logical conclusion   a

2. be driven by people's feelings and sensitivities   b

3. pursue your agenda, sometimes at the expense of others   c

4. treat each member of the meeting fairly and with respect   d

5. brace yourself to be able to face any conversation   e

Scenario 2: With your boss

When you are with your boss, which of these behaviours are you likely to use:

1. be more driven by his/her mood   b

2. be influenced by whether you are treated with respect   d
   and appropriate conduct

3. clearly present your case   a

4. adjust what you present knowing your boss's views   c
   on the subject

5. say what you were going to say, irrespective   e

Scenario 3: With your team

When you are meeting with your team, which of these behaviours are you likely to use:

1. go out of your way to treat everyone the same   d

2. insist the decisions reached are supported by good   a
   argument

3. give attention to those who agree with you so that   c
   your point of view wins

4. gain positive participation by being sensitive to   b
   how each feels

5. tell everyone to toughen up and speak openly   e

Scenario 4: With your peers

When meeting with your peers, which of these behaviours are you likely to use:

1. give priority to positively handling relationships   b
2. see some before the meeting in order to gain their support   c
3. rely on clarity of argument   a
4. be consistent, equally sharing information with all   d
5. just say what you were going to say, irrespective of what others feel   e

Scenario 5: With stakeholders

When interacting with key internal/external stakeholders, which of these behaviours are you most likely to use:

1. know how far you can influence each one in determining your outcomes   c
2. never take each person beyond their comfort zone   b
3. establish a way of operating that is fair for all   d
4. give priority to clarity of argument   a
5. be tough enough to face any conversation   e

Scenario 6: With clients

When meeting with important internal/external clients, which of
these behaviours are you most likely to use:

1. rely on presenting the facts in order to provide   a
    good service

2. establish how matters should be conducted   d
    emphasizing transparency

3. be influenced by the concerns and sensitivities   b
    of each client

4. be responsive to your clients' concerns in   c
    order to shape expectations your way

5. just speak the truth   e

Scenario 7: When making your case, do you

1. brace yourself to face comments, criticisms?   e

2. pay attention to the sentiments in the room   b
    and not offend?

3. do the right thing and be honest and transparent?   d

4. know how far you can take each person in the room   c
    in order to get your way?

5. draw on logic supported by evidence?   a

Scenario 8: Giving feedback (to your boss)

When giving feedback to your boss, which of these behaviours are you most likely to use:

1. state why the feedback is given and ask for permission to do so — d
2. simply list the issues in question — a
3. put a positive spin even if that is not the case — c
4. be conscious of how he/she will react before giving feedback — b
5. say what you feel and ask that he/she does likewise — e

Scenario 9: Giving feedback (to your subordinates)

When giving feedback to your subordinates, which of these behaviours are you most likely to use:

1. put a positive spin even if that is not the case — c
2. be conscious of how he/she will react before giving feedback — b
3. simply list the issues in question — a
4. state why the feedback is given and ask for permission to do so — d
5. say what you feel and ask that he/she do likewise — e

Scenario 10: Giving feedback (to your peers)

When giving feedback to your peers, which of these behaviours are you most likely to use:

1. simply list the issues in question   `a`

2. be conscious of how he/she will react before giving feedback   `b`

3. put a positive spin even if that is not the case   `c`

4. state why the feedback is given and ask for permission to do so   `d`

5. say what you feel and ask that he/she does likewise   `e`

Scenario 11: Making a presentation

In making a presentation, which of these behaviours are you most likely to use:

1. be popular by playing to the audience   `c`

2. do not deviate from what is right and proper to say   `d`

3. sequence your points in a clear and rational manner   `a`

4. feel what the audience wants to hear   `b`

5. have the courage to raise the uncomfortable issue   `e`

Scenario 12: At home

At home, which of these behaviours are you most likely to use:

1. no matter how tired, logically find ways through the concerns of each member of the family `a`

2. always show interest even though you are perceived as being insensitive `e`

3. know whom to please in order to get your way `c`

4. ensure that each has the right to speak before any important decision is taken `d`

5. no matter how tired, be rejuvenated by being with the family `b`

Scenario 13: Receiving feedback

When receiving feedback, which of these reactions are you more likely to have:

1. appreciate that the feedback is logically considered and presented `a`

2. recognize that the other person is sensitive to how you could react `b`

3. understand that the comments made are what the other person wants me to hear `c`

4. respect the fact that you are dealt with exactly the same as anybody else `d`

5. strengthen yourself emotionally to her what is to be said `e`

Scenario 14: In general

In general, do you rely more on:

1. the sensitivities of each person   b

2. logical argument   a

3. treating everyone the same   e

4. negotiating to your favour   c

5. being resilient to face up to any situation   d

Scoring instructions

Carefully transfer your scores (1 least likely – 5 most likely) into the table

	Score				
Scenario	IQ	EQ	PQ	RQ	MQ
1	a	b	c	e	d
2	a	b	c	e	d
3	a	b	c	e	d
4	a	b	c	e	d
5	a	b	c	e	d
6	a	b	c	e	d
7	a	b	c	e	d
8	a	b	c	e	d

	Score				
Scenario	IQ	EQ	PQ	RQ	MQ
9	a	b	c	e	d
10	a	b	c	e	d
11	a	b	c	e	d
12	a	b	c	e	d
13	a	b	c	e	d
14	a	b	c	e	d
TOTAL*					

* Cross-check: Total of five columns should add to 195

Interpreting your 5Qs score

Please note that the checklist on page 133 is not a psychometric test. Its main objective is to prompt further discussions on the 5Qs, and how rationalization processes and behavioural patterns affect leadership capabilities.

Here is the way to interpret your scores

Sum each column on the scoring table and look for highest mark (++) and secondhighest mark (+). Note that columns I, II, III, IV and V represent IQ, EQ, PQ, RQ MQ, respectively. Thus, for example, a highest mark for IQ will translate as IQ++; a secondhighest mark for IQ will translate into IQ+.

Definitions

IQ	The ability to acquire knowledge to resolve logical or strategic problems within a given context; reflects rational and deductive reasoning abilities.
EQ	The ability to understand and manage both their own emotions and those of others; understands how emotions influence objectivity and decision-making, and how this knowledge is used to build relationships and improve performance.
PQ	The ability to engage and influence stakeholders and affect the behaviour of others in order to navigate a way forward through diverse agendas, favourable to one's own agenda.
RQ	The ability to emotionally understand the tensions and pressures being faced and be realistic about what is required in order to sustain performance.
MQ	The ability to understand one's own value system and draw on this to determine the moral boundaries which guide behaviour and beyond which one will not transgress irrespective of the circumstances in order to resolve ethical dilemmas.

Guideline to interpreting your scores

IQ++

EQ+	Clear, rational, decisive whilst being sensitive to stakeholders, individuals and groups. Genuinely striving for shared and open participation.
PQ+	Clear, rational, decisive whilst being sensitive to particular stakeholders, individuals and groups from the perspective of selecting whom to influence to progress one's own agenda.
RQ+	Clear, rational, decisive and realistic about what is required in stretching circumstances to contribute.
MQ+	Clear rational decisive in order to establish moral and ethical boundaries between acceptable/unacceptable and right/wrong behaviours.

EQ++

IQ+	Constantly sensitive to stakeholders, individuals and groups in order to bring about shared and open participation through clearly providing the rational for such orientation.
PQ+	Particularly sensitive to only selected stakeholders, individuals and groups, drawing on flattery/charm to favourably influence the other parties to accept one's one needs/agendas.
RQ+	Sensitive to one's vulnerabilities and realistic about what is personally required to become emotionally strengthened.
MQ+	Constantly sensitive to stakeholders, individuals and groups, in order to guide others to adopt appropriate ethical/moral standards and ways of thinking

PQ++

IQ+	Particularly focused on influencing others to realize one's ends/agendas through positioning comments and arguments in a rational and logical manner favouring predetermined outcomes.
EQ+	Conscious of what is necessary to realize one's one ends/agendas, a sensitive interrelationship approach is adopted with stakeholders, individual and groups, so that others feel one's warmth and friendship and unwittingly adopt one's perspective.
RQ+	Conscious of the tensions, pressures and agendas in each context in order to be strengthened to work through these challenges.
MQ+	Conscious of what is necessary to realize one's aims/agendas, moral/ethical behaviour/high ground is adopted, so that others feel that what one suggests to do is the right thing to do.

RQ++

IQ+	Drawing on evidence and logic in order to realistically realize the nature of the challenges to be faced.

EQ+	Sensitive to one's own and others' vulnerabilities, enables a sharing of experiences and approaches in order to realize better engagement through being more resilient.
PQ+	Conscious of what is required to face up to challenges, the confidence to work through multiple agendas in order to realize one's own goals.
MQ+	Aware of the strength of character required to see through challenges provides the fortitude to ensure moral boundaries are maintained.
MQ++	
IQ+	Firm on ethical boundaries to adopt; rational and deductive argument is used to justify one's position.
EQ+	Firm on the ethical boundaries to adopt; sensitivity to stakeholders, individuals and groups is shown through mentoring and personal warmth in order to facilitate a shared view on appropriate conduct.
PQ+	Firm on the ethical boundaries to adopt; influence over particular stakeholders, individuals and groups is pursued through displaying sensitivity and warmth to only those relationships considered necessary to gain acceptance of one's own perspective of right/wrong, appropriate/inappropriate behaviour.
RQ+	Being firm on the ethical boundaries to maintain: recognition of what must be endured in order to have no compromise on these ethical standards.

INDEX